★SAVING Democracy

A Blueprint for a Better Society

★SAVING Democracy

A Blueprint for a Better Society

Adam Efron

Saving Democracy
By Adam Efron

Cover portrait by Dani Shavit.
Cover design and interior design and formatting by Elevation Press of Colorado.

All characters and events in this novel, other than those clearly in the public domain, are fictitious and any resemblance to real persons, living or dead, is purely coincidental.

The opinions expressed in this book are the author's own and do not reflect the views of Elevation Press of Colorado, its associated authors, or its principal employees.

efronadam49@gmail.com

ISBN 978-0-932624-21-5

1. Main category—[Politics & Social Sciences] 2. Other categories—[Politics & Government]—[Public Affairs & Policy]—[Social Policy]

ELEVATION PRESS
OF COLORADO

Cedaredge, Colorado
elevation-press-books.com

Table of Contents

About the Author

Adam Efron was born in a refugee camp in Poland but grew up in Israel. He became the eternal student by studying for twenty years after high school, with a student card in his pocket until the age of 40.

Adam received an Industrial Engineering certificate after completing a two-year course in Israel. He then studied Mechanical Engineering for one year at the Technion in Israel followed by Physics and Material Science at Iowa State University located in Ames, Iowa, United States. Later he studied for a PhD in the Nuclear Engineering Department at Beer Sheva University, Israel. Subsequently, he relocated to South Africa and lived there for sixteen years.

Adam co-authored four papers published in scientific magazines, summarizing his metallurgical research for his masters and doctoral degrees.

Adam has worked as a consultant to factories in Israel, increasing production four-fold with only half of the original staff. In South Africa, he entered a goldmine for the first time in his life, and, within three months, he instituted improved working methods for the drilling crews, who were then able to increase their production three-fold.

Ultimately, he worked as a consultant for many organizations in South Africa and implemented cost-saving methods, which overall saved them ten million Rand every year.

This hectic life exposed him to many ills in our democratic society, especially the role of lawyers in the existing legal system. In the 1970's, he already foresaw the end of Israeli democracy and has witnessed its gradual deterioration.

Chapter 1

Your Life in My Ideal Democracy

I am tired of politicians making promises and never fulfilling those promises.

I am tired of the legal system that does not protect me.

I am tired of lawyers who take advantage of my problems.

I am tired of big corporations that intimidate me.

I am tired of bad service.

I am tired of religious people imposing their standards on me.

I am tired of not knowing if or how an increasing number of new and so-called "wonderful" technologies work.

You have been conditioned to believe that the current democratic system was designed for the benefit of the masses.

You have been conditioned to believe that the current democratic system is not perfect, but that this is the best we can do.

You have been conditioned to believe that the legal system is not perfect, but that this is the best we can do.

You have been intimidated and made to believe that any change would be for the worse and that it might even destroy the existing system.

However, this is not the truth. Our current democratic system often benefits the few at the expense of the rest of us.

If you feel like me, I have thought-provoking and practical solutions for you. These solutions expose the nature of false conventions that have been imposed on us for the benefit of the few.

I am offering you simple solutions that can be easily implemented in our lifetime and will change your life and mine, enabling us to take back control of our lives.

If you feel like me, please read the following short summary of my proposals that are detailed in my book: *SAVING DEMOCRACY — A BLUEPRINT FOR A BETTER SOCIETY.*

I am inviting you to live with me in my new democracy.

You will start your democratic life on the day you are born. At birth, all your biometric data will be recorded, and no one will attempt to abduct you, because the abductor will be afraid, knowing that you can be found easily.

You will lie in your crib, safe in the knowledge that you have two parents who have received proper education as to how to bring you up, educate you and feed you correctly, while having the financial means to provide you with what you need. More importantly, you will know that your parents have taken the proper steps to ensure that they are compatible and will stay together at least until you are an independent adult.

You will start your academic education with 19 other kids like you. You will be greeted by two teachers, both of whom have at least a master's degree. They will earn at least twice the median salary in the country and will be free to teach you to use your intellect, so that you will not blindly accept any dogma without question, especially religious dogma. Your teachers will be proud of their profession and free to teach you in their own way, as long as you achieve the required academic goals.

At school you will not learn to be a winner, but you will learn to be the best you can be and be proud of it. You will not only be taught academic skills but will be prepared for the life ahead of you, and for the democratic society that you will be an integral part of.

In high school, you will receive drafts of new laws from Parliament or another democratic system, and you will evaluate them. You will decide whether the wording of these new laws is clear enough for everyone to understand.

And if, like most kids, you sometimes behave inappropriately, you will spend a day cleaning the streets adjacent to your school.

You will be at school 11.5 months a year, from 08:00 to 17:00 (that is, 8 a.m. to 5 p.m.) In school, you will learn many important life skills, as well as skills that will enable you to understand the political system that controls your life.

From the age of 18, you will vote for Parliament as well as other national leadership positions and for many other important positions, such as the committee for selecting ministerial candidates, and the head of the Judiciary

System. You will always vote from home. You will not go to rallies and cheer for politicians. You will sit at home with their resumes or curriculum vitae (CV's) and evaluate their suitability for the job. You will vote for the party of your choice through the internet and decide the order of the members that will be given a seat in Parliament. If you wish to vote for a new party and worry that your vote will be wasted if the party does not enter Parliament, don't worry, since you will also be able to vote for your second and/or third choice of party. Your second or third choice will be counted if your first choice of party did not receive enough votes to enter Parliament.

In Parliament, there will always be one ruling party with at least a 51% majority, so that the ruling party will be able to implement the policies for which it was elected.

Your ministers will be professionals and not politicians, so that they will know how to manage their ministries effectively. However, they will be required to implement the laws of the Parliament which **you** elected. (Similar conditions will apply to other democratic systems.)

 To ensure that you receive good service, every business whose products or services you wish to purchase or use, will be required to show you its rating from its clients, and similarly, every public servant will be required to show you a cumulative rating from the members of the public who have been served. You will also rate every business and service provider.

At work you will not feel exploited! You will know that your managing director and senior managers are probably earning more than you, but not excessively, and you will know that none of them is earning more than four times the median salary.

At work, if you encounter illegal or immoral behaviors by your managers, you will not be afraid to be a whistleblower. This will ensure that directors and owners of businesses are accountable for their actions and furthermore will not only serve private interests but also the public interest. As a result, your boss will not dare to instruct you to do anything illegal or immoral, and you will not be compelled to do anything illegal or immoral in order to keep your job.

The same standards will be applied to public offices.

Your contract with your employer, your landlord, or any other company, will be standard government issue, and will take care of the interests of both sides.

Every product that you buy will have **all** the relevant information displayed clearly. Where was it bought? How much did the seller pay for it? What are its shortcomings?

Your banking and insurance costs will be much lower, your retirement pension will be much higher, and you will be secure in knowing that your interests are being taken care of, as your bank, your insurance company and your pension fund will be nonprofit organizations. Furthermore, you can rest assured that no other client gets more privileges than you, since you will know everything that the bank's employees do with every client, and **you** will not only elect the managing director, but will also have the power to dismiss that director.

When you fall in love and decide to get married, you will be required to undergo counseling, which will ensure that you understand that marriage is not just about sex, but that it is a serious commitment requiring many difficult compromises.

When you decide to have a child, you and your spouse will be required to have relevant counseling to ensure that you both understand the complexities of bringing up a child. Furthermore, the counselor will help you to assess whether or not you have the means to provide the child with what he or she needs.

The legal system, which is arguably the greatest scourge of our modern life, will be user-friendly. All lawyers will be government employees. Everybody will have access to identical legal services, whether it is you or a tycoon or a large corporation. Going to court for a just cause will cost you nothing. Getting legal advice will be charged at the actual cost to the state.

The foregoing are highlights from the 53 chapters of my book which offer solutions to many situations which may be affecting you negatively. If you enact my solutions, you will be empowered and will have much more control over all aspects of your life.

Chapter 2

Introduction

Why should a presumably sane person, who is not a professor of political science, get up one morning and decide to write a book detailing his proposals for correcting the existing democratic system?

I grew up in Israel in the 1950's, when the country's fledgling democracy was struggling to absorb immigrants from all over the world and to establish a democracy which would serve and be acceptable to all its citizens. Initially, like so many others, I naively believed in the integrity and morality of my fellow countrymen and in my country's democracy. However, from an early age, I often encountered what I considered to be immoral behavior, which I felt undermined the basic tenets of society.

I strongly believe that a sense of morality, i.e., showing consideration for the other, is the cohesive force that binds every society together, and I believe that its absence will corrode this cohesive force and will result in rampant corruption which can destroy a country over time. Rampant corruption has destroyed empires, most recently the Turkish Empire at the end of the First World War, and it will also destroy existing democracies if we do not do anything to stop it.

One example of this lack of morality occurred when I was a teenager working as a cashier in a movie theatre. I was working with an elderly man whom I admired, since he was one of the pioneers who had fought to establish the new State of Israel. One day when he came to work, I noticed that he was very annoyed. When I asked him why he was annoyed, he told me that the hubcaps on his car had been stolen. I sympathized with him, but when I asked what he had done about it, he replied, "Well of course, I took the hubcaps from another car in the street!"

Incidents like this have stayed with me to this day and have gradually alienated me from Israeli society. I am sharing this personal experience with you in order to convey my attitude towards immorality and corruption.

In my view there is no such thing as "a minor infraction" because these minor infractions inevitably lead to more serious crimes.

I spent twenty years of my life studying science and engineering with a student I.D. in my wallet until the age of 40. My education enabled me to develop many important skills, including critical thinking skills. I spent five years studying and doing research at Iowa State University in the USA. For seven years I worked in a research facility in Israel doing research towards a PhD degree. For sixteen years I worked as a consultant, reducing costs in South African companies while also working as a volunteer police reservist which exposed me further to the ills of society and to the shortcomings of various aspects of the democratic system. My work as an industrial engineer tasked with improving efficiency in Israeli factories also influenced my views of society and democracy.

Sadly, nowadays, the United States, Israel and South Africa are rated as flawed democracies with similarly low ratings. From my personal experience, I would question whether Israel and South Africa can even be classified as democracies at all. So, what does this say about American democracy?

There is a consensus that the existing democratic system is the best possible option, even with its many shortcomings, and that any major change might impact negatively on its very foundations. As you will see in this book, I have decided to reject this consensus, and propose alternatives that, in my opinion, will remedy the existing troubling and potentially dangerous situation.

What motivated me to start writing down my ideas? I was inspired to start writing this book because of the glaring flaws in the present **legal system**, which has a profound impact on both our quality of life and on our democratic rights. I know that many people despise lawyers, but we are locked into the belief that, like democracy, the existing legal system is the least of all evils.

There are so many glaring examples of the gross injustice of the existing legal system. One such example is the common practice of police officers or prosecutors closing files at their discretion or making a deal with the accused to plead to a lesser charge. As a result, the victim is victimized once again. Therefore, in my book, I propose changes that will remedy the present flawed situation by altering the role that lawyers play in the legal system.

I believe that the time has come to take a good look at the existing legal system and push for a radical change. The present legal system is a travesty of our democratic rights. It needs to be overhauled, so that justice is accessible to everyone, regardless of their financial circumstances.

In Chapter 17 *(Courts and Judges—The Legal System)*, I present my proposals to change the existing legal system. I come up with working solutions, which will put the victim of the crime first, rather than focusing on the rights of the accused.

However, the more I thought about the flaws in the existing legal system and about a better legal system that takes care of the rights of every citizen, the more I realized that I also needed to address all other aspects of the democratic system, because all these aspects are closely interconnected.

While I was thinking about my proposals to improve the democratic system, I realized that, without major changes to **children's education**, there is no chance that a new system will be established and survive in the long term.

Children absorb the norms and values of their family during their formative years, followed by the influence of the country's culture or lack thereof. Obviously, the school system is an integral part of the child's development, so dictators throughout history have used the school system to influence society. A stark example of this is Adolf Hitler's success in raising a generation of fanatic killers through education, in only 12 years.

Further proof of the long-lasting effect of early education on children, is the fact that almost all the children in a Muslim country follow the Muslim faith and almost all children in a Christian country follow Christianity for all their lives. Once children absorb certain norms and beliefs, these concepts will stay with them for the rest of their lives. Even the most gifted children cannot escape from this unhealthy influence. Isaac Newton, the brilliant scientist, remained religious for all his life, and it adversely affected his work. There are many such examples of the adverse effects of brainwashing on children. We have seen the consequences most recently when the US failed in its attempt to bring democracy to Islamic countries in the Middle East, even though they would have benefited greatly, as was the case with Germany and Japan after the Second World War.

Another issue that I address in my book is what makes people elect politicians who have failed them repeatedly. The answer is lack of morality and bad education as well as the realization that is sadly often true, that the alternative is no better. This is a society that has lost its soul and undoubtedly is a sad reflection of the existing educational system. Similarly, why do people continue believing and supporting religions that have never given them any tangible or proven benefits? This is the result of religious leaders successfully brainwashing their followers.

There are other ills in society that originate from the educational system, such as unhealthy competition, that is the result of the flawed principle of winners and losers.

I studied at university in the US during the Reagan era, and I loved every minute of it. However, as early as my sophomore year; I was surprised when many American students came to me for help with their studies, even in English classes although this was not my mother tongue. Later I realized that American students approached me since they did not help each other. They had been educated according to the principle of winners and losers, so they were conditioned to think that helping other students would hurt their standing in the class. In my opinion, this attitude turns everybody into a loser. If kids grow up with a spirit of cooperation, we shall all be winners.

I have mentioned changes to the **legal system** and the **educational system**. Next, we need to look at the **citizens' involvement** in various aspects of running the country.

Currently, in most democratic countries, people vote, or do not vote, once every four or five years and most of them are not involved in major decisions, except occasionally going on a march to protest about a specific issue. This compliance can be partially understood by people's tendency to accept that the people in power know better than they do and/or their disillusionment with the existing system.

However, I would like to remind you that many important and well-educated people in Germany (industrialists), in the United Kingdom (some members of the royal family), and many in the United States (like Charles Lindbergh and others), made the mistake of supporting Hitler. Similarly, in the First World War, where there were no clear objectives and logical reasons for starting the conflict, people went to war with great enthusiasm, without understanding the shortsightedness of their politicians' decisions.

It is my goal to empower every citizen to have an impact on many more major decisions than is currently the case.

The next major issue I deal with in my book is the way Parliament passes laws. (I am using Parliament as my main example, but you can also consider my thoughts to apply likewise to the American Congress.)

If a Parliament member, with good intentions, has an idea for a law which will solve a critical problem, the new law might not achieve its desired goals for any one of the following reasons:

- The law has not been researched properly.
- It was not written with enough precision.
- The minister ignores it.
- The treasury does not allocate the required budget.
- A parliamentary committee transfers the budget to be used for other purposes.
- The police do not enforce it.

In such a situation, the Parliament member can take the credit for passing the law, despite the fact that the law does not achieve its goal. In Israel, for example, there are very impressive laws restricting smoking in public places, but these laws were not researched and worded properly. As a result, I challenge you to find an entrance to a business building or a bus stop with a roof, or an open air restaurant with a roof where you will not be surrounded by smokers, even though it is against the law and, as a result, 800 Israelis die annually from inhaling passive smoke.

Another cornerstone of a vibrant democracy is a free, professional and **independent news media** whose task is to be the watchdog of the democracy. When the news media is money-driven and owned or financed by wealthy individuals or large corporations, the news media inevitably serves their interests rather than the public interest.

I envision a responsible citizen who reads a reliable newspaper every day and spends part of each day evaluating his or her representatives and their decisions. I believe that, if people are exposed to objective news reporting, they will better understand the problems plaguing their country. They will then have the tools to evaluate options in order to choose the most suitable solutions to problems which also take their interests into account.

In my proposals, I ensure that citizens will be much better informed so that they will be able to be involved in making many more important decisions than nowadays. Furthermore, these decisions will be based on more objective information because they will be based on completely independent news media sources.

In my introduction, I have presented examples from my experience while living in Israel. In contrast, American democracy seemed to be resilient until recently. However, the Donald Trump era exposed America's inherent weaknesses and showed how fragile its democracy is. Trump embodied the principle of winning at all costs, and the consequences could be clearly seen.

To summarize, it is my goal to give you and every other ordinary citizen more power over government decisions, so that you do not have to rely so much on the professional and moral integrity of our leaders, because history has shown us that they are not infallible. Similarly, I aim to reduce the self-serving influence and control that powerful people and large organizations currently have over decisions made by the government, since their goal is to promote their interests at the expense of the average citizen.

In the 53 chapters of my book, I cover many aspects of life in a democratic state and offer solutions that will correct the flaws, and even more importantly, will make the state less vulnerable to becoming non-democratic.

If this introduction was too lengthy for you, I apologize. I am now inviting you to visit my ideal democratic state. Peek in and see if you like it and if you want to live with me in this state.

Chapter 3

Principles for a Democratic State

How can we make our democratic state work for us now, and more importantly make it continue working for us in the future? The following are my basic principles for establishing a strong and resilient democratic state whose institutions and businesses will actually serve the people.

1. Citizenship conditional on acceptance and obedience to all state laws.
2. Citizens' perpetual involvement in public life.
3. Citizens kept up to date with reliable and current information.
4. Online voting system for Parliamentary elections and all other mandated elections.
5. Only citizens with suitable qualifications can serve as ministers or congressmen. Ministers should be the highest qualified professionals in the country in their field, and not the most powerful and/or popular politicians.
6. Limited number of terms for all ministers.
7. Limited number of terms for all politicians.
8. Parliamentary positions should be conditional on minimum age and education i.e., at least forty years old and in possession of a university degree.
9. Politicians are not allowed any involvement in their private enterprises. Similarly, they cannot make decisions regarding companies that might have influence on their private interests.
10. More public officials elected directly by the public to ensure better separation of powers.
11. Free access to all information concerning the activities of all public servants.
12. Removal of all non-democratic forces from public life.
13. Acceptance of the notion that religion is a non-democratic force, and must be removed from public life, from the legislature and,

most importantly, from children's schools and all other public educational institutions.

14. Acceptance of the concept that truth in public life is another cornerstone of democracy and a healthy society. Prosecution of all disseminators of fake news and lies, including lies in parliament, government and the legal system.

15. Telling the truth to police officers and in court should be compulsory for ordinary citizens and especially lawyers.

16. Lawyers only allowed to present facts known to them, and not allowed to present a fictitious "line of defense."

17. Termination of client-lawyer confidentiality.

18. Cost-free and equal legal protection in court for everyone.

19. No private lawyers. Only public legal services at nominal fees allowed.

20. Independent media is an important cornerstone of democracy, without which it cannot survive. All news media services must act as nonprofit organizations. They must be free from any private or political pressure.

21. High-quality, compulsory, cost free, liberal and non-religious educational system for the children of all citizens, from the age of 3 to 18.

22. State-controlled, free and equal healthcare services for all citizens.

23. Establishment of a separate police force and prosecutor's office, that is independent of the government and elected directly by the public. Their function will be to protect the public from abuse of power by corrupt politicians, ministers, judges, police, and all other public servants. (See Chapter 19: A Separate Police Force and Prosecution Department.)

24. Directors of private companies bear criminal responsibility for their organizations' illegal actions. Compulsory prosecution of any director whose company is fined by the government, irrespective of the reason.

25. Private organizations should be limited in size, because very large corporations can use their power to influence and intimidate the government.

26. Owners of all private organizations responsible for establishing functioning independent local labor unions. Similarly, all ministers responsible for ensuring that every public office has a local labor union.
27. No right to strike for employees working in monopolies.
28. Legal protection for whistleblowers in public and private organizations.
29. Ongoing public supervision of all private enterprises and public offices.
30. Establishment of banking, insurance services and pension funds as publicly supervised non-profit organizations.
31. Cap on salaries. The highest salaries in private and government organizations related to the median salary in their organization or in the country.
32. Special status for police officers and teachers in terms of public respect.
33. Reasonable minimum salary for police officers and teachers.
34. Prosecution for having financial interaction with criminals including paying for racketeering, paying criminals for any services or paying ransom money.
35. Community public works for purchasing illegal drugs.
36. Only selected immigrants allowed into the country, even if they are refugees.

Chapter 4

The Constitution

The constitution of a democratic country is, and should be, a vital cornerstone of a healthy democracy. The constitution is made up of a set of laws enacted by Parliament. If Parliament wishes to change any of these laws, it requires more than a 51% majority.

The constitution exists:

Firstly, to safeguard minorities from abuse by the ruling party.

Secondly, it exists to safeguard previously accepted principles from arbitrary changes by the ruling party.

The constitution must also include safeguards against forces that can destroy democracy e.g., religious leaders, power hungry politicians, non-democratic political parties and large corporations. Furthermore, it must also safeguard the freedom and independence of the news media.

The following are my enumerated recommendations for additions to the existing constitution in my ideal democratic state:

1. Any change to the constitution will require a 75% majority in Parliament, and subsequently 66% majority in a national referendum.
2. A citizen can serve as a Member of Parliament for no more than three terms in a lifetime i.e., a maximum of 15 years in total, not necessarily consecutively. Every citizen can serve as the Prime Minister for no more than two terms i.e., 10 years in a lifetime, not necessarily consecutively.
3. Every citizen can serve as a minister for no more than four terms in a lifetime, i.e., 20 years in total, but having served in a ministerial position, such a citizen can never serve as a Member of Parliament. This ruling does not include the Prime Minister.
4. All ministers must be professionals in their field, and selected by a professional committee, with the exception of the Prime Minister, who will be an elected politician.

5. The value of any private organization should not be allowed to exceed 3% of the annual national budget of the state. Furthermore, no individual should be allowed to own or control private businesses whose total value exceeds 3% of the annual national budget.

6. Parliament must be responsible for ensuring the existence of an independent news media, which is free from any pressure from the government or from any religious, private individual, or corporate influence.

7. There must be complete separation between state and religion, including a ban on religious practices in the public domain, and a ban on religious leaders from participating in the democratic process or influencing others regarding their voting choice in any democratic election.

8. The constitution must also include a ban on religious leaders or religious professionals from influencing the public or private schooling system.

9. The state should be prohibited from financing or subsidizing religious practices or institutions either directly or indirectly.

Chapter 5

Citizenship

Citizenship should not be considered to be a "God-Given Right."

Citizenship should come with responsibilities, whereby the state takes care of the individual, and in return, the individual has obligations towards the state. Citizens who do not honor their obligations towards the state should have their citizenship revoked.

However, if you, the citizen, honor your obligations to the state, you will gain control over all aspects of managing the state, and, as a result, your quality of life will improve.

The following are my enumerated recommendations:

1. All citizens and residents will wear a government issued name-tag on their chest, with name and city of residence clearly indicated. From the age of 13, all young people will receive this name tag, and will always wear it on their chest when outside of their residence. The reasoning behind this is that a name-tag breaks down boundaries between people, and more importantly, it enables easier identification of both perpetrators of anti-social and criminal behavior.

2. All visitors to the country will also be issued with a name-tag, showing their name and country of origin.

3. Every member of society, including all citizens, residents, children from day of birth, tourists, and visitors to the country will have their biometric data on record. This will make it much easier for the police to identify offenders and criminals and as a result be able to solve crimes much easier.

4. Every citizen who adopts a pet will have that pet registered, and the animal's biometric data recorded by the state. This will help the police to identify lost pets and even criminals, since they might leave biometric data of their pet in the scene of the crime. Moreover, if the citizen does not clean up after their pet, the pet and that pet's owner can be easily identified.

5. At the age of 18, every young person will have to sign a declaration stating that he or she has no objections to obeying the laws of the country, including objections of a religious nature. Anyone refusing to sign such a declaration will automatically lose their citizenship.

6. Any citizen who refuses to obey the law for religious reasons will lose their citizenship.

7. Voting will be compulsory! Any citizen who does not vote three times consecutively in any kind of election where voting is compulsory by law, will lose citizenship unless he or she can present a valid reason that is beyond their control. Citizenship comes with obligations and fulfilling the obligation to vote is one of them (see Chapter 5: *Citizenship*.)

8. Residents who are not citizens will not benefit from any privileges reserved for citizens, such as social security and The National Health Service. However, their children will be required to attend school, like all citizens' children, but they will have to pay for the cost of their schooling.

Chapter 6

Parliamentary System

Introduction

You live in a democratic country. Are you dissatisfied? Do you see flaws in the system? Are you despondent with the quality and/or performance of your representatives? Do you feel that your life could be better? If your answer is YES, in this chapter you will find an alternative parliamentary system that will work better for you.

A democratic country does not need professional politicians who have based their income solely on political activity. A democratic parliament should be composed of citizens who are experienced and accomplished professionals in their field, who have agreed to devote a certain period of their life to serving their country. Even according to the Bible, only the useless want to rule (as stated in the Yotam Allegory — Book of Judges, Chapter 8, Verse 7) and the ruler will abuse his power (The First Book of Samuel, Chapter 8, Verse 11.) We don't need them. Time and time again, we see how professional politicians covet their seats of power at all costs, and, consequently, cause a lot of harm to the citizens of their country.

For example, there is a small country in the Middle East called Israel that is theoretically democratic. The Israeli Government is composed of 26 ministers, with many additional vice ministers, almost all of whom have no clue about their ministerial duties. Actually, some of them do not even have any secular education at all.

In Israel, ministers and all civil servants are appointed by politicians. They are not appointed on the basis of relevant education and experience, but because of nepotism and political relationships. In Israel, you would be hard-pressed to find the most qualified and experienced professionals in positions of power. Furthermore, I cannot recall when any public servant or minister was dismissed for incompetence or failure to perform his or her duties or achieve their goals.

Moreover, the Israeli political system enables politicians who have been in jail to return to a ministerial or parliamentary position, sometimes even the same position they held before they were prosecuted for corruption or related charges. This is why ministerial appointments should not be left completely to the discretion of politicians.

Another problem concerning the appointments of public servants is the issue of the human psyche. Very few officials will appoint somebody under them who is more capable than they are. So, if ministers with limited abilities are appointed, we can be sure those officials will do their utmost to prevent more capable people from working under them, even if this is detrimental to the performance of their office.

We can also clearly see the flaws in the American parliamentary system, which embodies a powerful president and two elected bodies, a senate and a house. The system is potentially dysfunctional when the two bodies have a different majority party. For example, we saw how President Barack Obama failed to implement policies, promised to the citizens for their benefit, like an omnibus health care system, although he was elected on the basis of these promises. This was because of dissension between the US Senate and the US House of Representatives.

We can conclude from the above examples that the existing democratic system suffers from various shortcomings, and we have to completely revise the whole political system to remedy at least the following shortcomings:

1. Every young person can make politics a profession, irrespective of his or her qualifications.
2. Politicians too often make empty promises which they do not intend to fulfill.
3. Politicians receive private financial support which makes them indebted to their financiers.
4. Many politicians spend much of their time in office ensuring their reelection instead of doing the job they were elected for and serving the public.
5. Citizens choose candidates based on empty and shallow speeches.

6. After the elections, citizens discover that very little has changed, and besides complaining over coffee with friends, there is very little they can do about it.

7. Politicians appoint ministers based on personal relationships, or based on admiration for former generals, but often not based on their qualifications, knowledge of management and expertise and experience related to their office.

To those who believe the urban legend that a minister does not have to be an expert, I answer:

1. "Would you appoint this person to manage your private business?"

2. Managers do not appoint better qualified subordinates, fearing that they will show them up. Thus, unqualified ministers ensure a low level of management in their ministries.

My revisions to the Parliamentary system:

First point, we need to ensure that our ministers are professionals in their fields. Moreover, the governing parliamentary party needs to ensure that these chosen ministers agree with their policies and will agree to implement them. Both these goals can be achieved by limiting Parliament's choices for ministers to a short list of qualified professionals and not party members.

Second point, a parliamentary system that is composed of many small parties is as bad as a system with only two parties. But irrespective of the number of parties in Parliament, there should be one party which represents the largest number of voters and has sufficient members of Parliament to implement the policies for which it was elected.

Third point, the legislative process led by the largest political party in Parliament needs to be separated from the managerial task of the ministers in implementing these laws and running the country.

Fourth point, we should select our political leaders in the same way that businesses select their staff i.e., based on their previous achievements. Unfortunately, the existing political system enables charismatic leaders to impress and influence the public with their personality, irrespective of their qualifications. This flaw enables people to make politics their lifetime career and their only source of income. As a result, we are stuck with politicians who have inadequate qualifications for ministerial positions. In the business sector, we do not go to rallies and cheer our employees as we do during the election process. We look at their resumes or CV's (curriculum vitae.) We listen to their answers to our questions, and then select the best and most qualified candidate. The same attitude can and should be applied to the political elections and appointments since all public servants are in fact **our employees**. We can implement my **proposed new system** since new technology (the internet) enables all citizens to participate easily in the democratic process and select various public servants from the comfort of their homes.

Fifth point, we must prevent various undemocratic groups, including religious professionals, who by their own admission do not acknowledge the authority of democratically elected leaders, to influence the political process and even to become part of it.

The sixth point is to stop private donations to political parties and candidates. Each party will receive the same election budget irrespective of their number of political candidates. At present, a political candidate needs the financial backing of generous donors in order to launch an election campaign. As a result, after being elected, the politician will be indebted to such financiers and undoubtedly serve them, rather than the public interest.

The seventh point is the continuous compulsory participation of **all qualified** voters in the democratic process. They do so not only by voting for parliament but also by voting for various public officials, as well as continuously evaluating and rating the services they receive from public officials. This is essential to preserve democracy and improve its efficiency. Nowadays citizens in the democratic state enjoy the benefits bestowed on them by the state. However, they must understand that by not voting they relinquish their right to influence the democratic process and enable sinister forces to influence Parliament and the government to benefit themselves at the expense of the ordinary citizen. **The state must force all qualified citizens to be active participants in this process.**

The eighth point is to ensure the existence of a reliable and financially independent news media since it is an essential cornerstone of any democracy. A reliable and independent news media is the main source of information used by the citizen to understand the political process and to shape informed opinion. Therefore, it is crucial that the news media will not be controlled by private money. In order to preserve democracy, it is crucial to separate the news media from private money.

The ninth point is that only citizens who have sufficient literacy skills to read the newspaper in the official language will be allowed to vote. This will prevent the phenomenon of voters, who do not have enough reliable information, from making an uninformed choice because of their lack of language skills. This will also prevent them from being influenced by others who do not have their best interests at heart.

The tenth point is to ensure that all activities of public servants are video recorded and put online, with a few exceptions that will be determined by an independent judiciary system.

The eleventh point is *the million-dollar question:* How many members should be in Parliament? I don't have a clear view on this subject. However, in my proposed system, the Parliament members will have to spend a lot of time preparing new laws, and we, the citizens, will know how much time they spend doing actual work. Therefore, I believe that the public that employs them should decide on the number of Parliament members. (See recommendation 16 in *Elections for Parliament*.)

In this chapter, I set out a new system that, in my opinion, will rectify the shortcomings in the existing democratic system. The new system is presented in detail to ensure that its implementation will not be hampered or jeopardized by hostile forces. However, before we delve into the details, I want to present to you a short summary of the system that will serve as a guideline in understanding my proposed system.

My proposed system is based on the following:
Parliament members

Citizens who wish to be members of parliament must be at least 40 years old, must send a detailed curriculum vita (CV) (see Chapter 30: Application for Employment in a Public Office) to the voting public, and can only serve in Parliament for a limited number of terms.

The qualified voter

To qualify for voting, a citizen must have full command of the official language, so as to be able to read newspapers.

Voting

Every **qualified voter** will vote from the **comfort of his or her home**:
- For a choice of 25 committee members who will select candidates for ministerial posts.
- For the party of the voter's choice, based on all the information from all the parties and from newspaper articles.
- The voter will put the members of the chosen party in order of preference. As a result, the parliament members will be those with the highest number of votes from the voters who voted for that particular party.
- The voter will also be called upon to vote on many other issues.

All the above process of getting information and voting is made possible due to the new technologies that are available today.

The committee for selecting candidates for ministers

The committee of 25 members will be elected by the public, based on their CV's prior to the parliamentary elections (see Chapter 30: *Application for Employment in a Public Office.*) The committee will select 5-10 of the most suitable candidates for each of the twelve ministerial positions. Ministers will be the most qualified professionals in the country for their ministerial position and cannot be politicians.

Every selected candidate for a ministerial position will receive a salary in the meantime and will have access to ministerial files, so that the candidate can prepare plans, goals and the required budget, and then wait until a new parliament has been elected.

Parliamentary Elections

Every party will get the **same budget** for the Parliamentary elections as well as equal access to the media, irrespective of the party's size. Every party will send information to all voters including detailed curriculum vitae (CV's) of all their members (see Chapter 30: *Application for Employment in a Public Office*.) Furthermore, the election committee will send every voter the newspapers of his or her choice, with articles about the elections.

In order to protect democracy, religious or non-democratic parties will not be allowed to participate in the democratic process. Every qualified citizen **must** vote from home through the internet. Each voter will elect the party of choice and decide in what order to list the party members.

In order to prevent the potential for fraud, the votes will be recorded in three computer centers via two independent transmission methods.

Furthermore, every citizen can use a personal code to check that each vote has been registered correctly.

In order to prevent the existence of too many small parties in parliament, a party will not be able to enter parliament unless it has received enough votes to secure four seats (out of 120) in Parliament in the first round of elections. However, to alleviate the voter's fear of a vote being wasted if the party of choice does not pass the threshold, each voter can vote for more than one party, and if the party of choice has not received enough votes to enter Parliament, the vote will be transferred to the second or third choice.

Parliament with one ruling party

No organization can be managed efficiently by a committee. Similarly, there must be only one ruling party in Parliament. Therefore, at least 51% of members **must** belong to the ruling party, so that Parliament can implement its policies.

If no party gets 51% of the votes, there will be a second round of elections between the two largest parties. The winning party will be assigned 51% of parliamentary members, and the number of members of all other parties will be reduced accordingly. The leading party will be able to carry out its policies alone or enter a coalition with another party. However, that other party will not be in a position to extort unreasonable demands from the leading party.

After the elections, members of Parliament for each party will be selected according to the number of votes they have received from the voters for their party in the first round of elections. With this system, the party itself will not decide who will represent them in Parliament as is the common practice at present.

Ministers elected by Parliament

Once the elected Parliament decides on its budget, the candidates for ministerial positions who have been shortlisted by the committee for selecting ministers, will amend their plans accordingly, and then will be interviewed by Parliament, who will choose the most suitable candidate for each ministerial position.

Prime minister

The Prime Minister will be a member of the largest party in Parliament who received the highest number of votes from party voters. The Prime Minister will not be elected by fellow party members.

Conclusion

Once you understand the logic of my system, you might wonder how come it has not been proposed up to now. The answer is very simple. It does not serve our politicians, tycoons or religious leaders. It serves you!

My goals to be achieved by recommendations enumerated below are:

    a. Full participation of all **literate** citizens in the democratic process.

    b. Voting by all literate citizens from the comfort of their own home.

    c. Citizens decide on the politicians from each party who will enter parliament.

    d. Ministers and parliament members are elected based on their qualifications and their views, and not on their public speaking skills.

    e. Limited number of terms for all politicians, ministers and the Prime Minister.

    f. Limited number of ministries, managed by the most qualified, non-political professionals in the country.

g. Prevention of any religious influence on the democratic process and on public servants, and total prohibition of non-democratic and/or religious professionals from participating in the democratic process.

h. Total prohibition of any financial influence on the parliamentary process.

i. Easy access for new parties to the democratic process.

j. One ruling party in Parliament.

The **existing democratic system** is based on idealistic principles designed to rectify the ills of previous autocratic systems. However, its idealism makes it vulnerable to anti-democratic forces. My system is designed to ensure that the will of the majority will prevail. Minorities will still be protected, but this protection will not allow them to circumvent and destroy the principles of the democratic system.

The following recommendations are designed to rectify issues inherent in the existing democratic system:

Citizens qualified to vote

1. Only citizens that are able to read a newspaper in the official language will be qualified to vote.

2. All high school seniors will be required to pass a literacy test in the **official language** that will prove their ability to read and understand written newspapers and then he or she will receive a Language Competency Certificate.

3. Citizens that are not in possession of a language competency certificate from high school will not be qualified to vote unless they pass a literacy exam. The exam will include reading newspaper articles, on which the citizen will have to answer questions in writing to demonstrate the ability to understand the articles. These exams will be done through the internet. Occasionally, citizens will be summoned to a face-to-face test to prevent fraud.

4. Voting will be **compulsory** for every citizen over 18 who has passed a Language Competency Test in the official language. If a citizen

does not vote that citizen will receive a large fine and will have to complete a specified number of hours of public works wearing a jacket specifying the reason. Exceptions will be made if the citizen has a compelling reason preventing him or her from voting. Not voting three times in a row, without a justified reason, will result in the loss of citizenship.

5. Prisoners, people with limited mental capacity, either from birth, or because of diminished mental capacity, and current residents of mental hospitals, or asylums, will not have the right to vote.
6. Citizens will vote through the internet from the comfort of their homes.
7. Every citizen will be identified by a code, similar to the system used to access any other secure site like a bank account, etc.
8. Citizens residing outside the country for a continuous period of more than 12 months will not be allowed to vote.

The committee for selecting ministerial candidates

1. A **professional committee** of 25 members will be elected by the citizens. Their duty will be to select and shortlist the most suitable candidates for ministerial positions. This will take place approximately a year before the parliamentary elections.
2. Elections for the new committee will be handled by the previous committee that selected candidates for ministers in the previous elections. For the first elections in this new system, the clerks who will be responsible for handling the paperwork will be appointed by the head of legal system.
3. The curriculum vitae (CV) of all the applicants for the new committee will be available to the public, similar to every other public servant. (See Chapter 30: *Application for Employment in a Public Office.*)
4. Parliament members and ministers, past or present, members of political parties and/or candidates for Parliament, or anyone else affiliated to a political party, will not be allowed to apply.

5. All the activities related to the committee will be open to the public via closed circuit video recording and available to the public online.

6. Every applicant for the new committee, like every public servant, will sign a document stating that he or she will never be influenced by religious considerations in the performance of his or her duties in public service. Any breach of this will be punished by at least five years of public works.

7. Religious professionals, citizens supplying religious services now or in the past, will not be allowed to submit their candidacy for the committee or any other position in the democratic process, including any government or parliamentary position.

8. All citizens who are qualified to vote will receive the detailed curriculum vitae (CV) of the candidates through the internet. (See Chapter 30: *Application for Employment in a Public Office*.) They will be able to submit oral or written questions to the candidates through the internet. They will have to vote through the internet for **25** candidates of their choice.

9. All voters must ensure that their selection of 25 candidates will include experts with knowledge and understanding of the qualifications required for each of the 12 ministerial positions. That is to say that, ideally, at least two members of the committee should have expertise suitable for understanding the requirements of each of the 12 ministerial positions.

10. The 25 candidates who have received the most votes will constitute the new committee for shortlisting candidates for ministerial positions.

11. The previous committee will be replaced by the new committee.

12. Once the new committee has been established, it will start the process of interviewing candidates who have submitted their detailed curriculum vitae (CV) for one of the 12 ministerial positions. (See Chapter 30: *Application for Employment in a Public Office*.)

13. The committee will be allowed to consult with experts to help them select the most suitable candidates for each of the 12 ministerial positions.

The selection of candidates for the 12 ministerial positions by the 25-member committee

1. The government will consist of 12 professional ministers plus the Prime Minister (see the section on Prime Minister.).
2. All government ministers will be professionals in their respective fields of expertise, having been selected and shortlisted by the elected committee.
3. Each of the twelve professional ministers cannot serve more than four terms in a lifetime and can never become a Member of Parliament.
4. The committee will short list 5-10 candidates for each of the twelve ministerial positions.
5. The shortlisted candidates for each ministerial position will get a salary, a budget and access to relevant ministerial files, and will be required to prepare their work plans with their required budget, goals and timetable for achieving these goals.
6. The shortlisted candidates will have to wait for the appointment of the newly elected Parliament **and its decision on its new budget**.

Political Parties

1. The Parliament will consist of 120 members with at least 61 members belonging to one party. The total number of members of Parliament can be different based on the population or other considerations, but this will not affect the proposed system.
2. Elections for Parliament will be every five years.
3. For the elections, each party will submit a list of candidates in order of preference. However, the final order of its members that will enter Parliament will be decided by the voter (see recommendation 3.)
4. Each candidate in every party will submit and publish a detailed and complete curriculum vitae (CV.) (See Chapter 30: *Application for Employment in a Public Office.*)
5. Any omission on a CV that is intended to deceive the public will be a criminal offence, punishable with at least five years public works.

Any other omission will disqualify him or her for the position and for any public office for life.

6. All candidates for Parliament must be at least 40 years old with at least a college education.

7. No candidate can have a criminal record, nor can a candidate be under criminal investigation, or involved in a civil case requiring costs paid to the state for litigating in bad faith.

8. No candidate can stand who has held at any time in the past a position in a religious organization, for example a priest or a rabbi or an imam. Similarly, the candidate cannot stand who has provided religious services and/or is an active participant in any religious order.

9. Any party and its members cannot be affiliated to any religious organization either now or in the past.

10. All parliamentary candidates must also explain how they are qualified for the position.

11. Every candidate for Parliament must clearly state a position on various issues, and on which particular issues the candidate will not be willing to compromise. These commitments will be legally binding. Any violation of these commitments will lead to immediate dismissal from Parliament and subsequent prosecution.

12. Each party, including new parties, will have to submit a party manifesto setting out their policies that do not contradict the principles of democratic rule and will specify on which policies they will not compromise. These commitments will be legally binding.

13. A political party cannot have an agreement with another party about the transfer of excess votes since not **all** their voters might agree to this arrangement. However, if a reasonable method can be established for transferring excess votes of the party to the second choice of each voter, this would be acceptable.

14. A member of Parliament can serve no more than three terms in a lifetime, including terms as Prime Minister.

15. A citizen cannot serve both in Parliament and as a Minister in a lifetime, with the exception of the Prime Minister. However, a member of Parliament can serve a portion of three terms as Prime Minister.
16. No religious party or non-democratic one will be allowed to participate in the democratic process.
17. A party can be disqualified from the elections **only** if the current Parliament votes that it is religious or non-democratic with a 75% majority. This will be a free vote and not subject to party policy and will be followed by a 2/3 majority of the popular vote in a public referendum.
18. In order to register, a **new party** will have to collect 1% of signatures from the pool of eligible voters. Nowadays, with the use of the internet, this can be done without investing any money in the process.
19. All the existing parties and all the new parties will receive the same budget and free access to the media, irrespective of the number of its members in the previous Parliament.

Elections for Parliament

1. Politicians will be forbidden from taking any private donations or using their own money, in pursuit of a parliamentary position.
2. Before the elections, every citizen who is qualified to vote will receive all the information from all the parties, detailed curriculum vitae (CV) of all their members (see Chapter 30: *Application for Employment in a Public Office.*). Every citizen will also receive articles about their members from at least two newspapers of the members' choice via the internet and/or by mail.
3. Every qualified citizen will elect the party of that citizen's choice through the internet **and list the candidates in the chosen party, in order of preference**.
4. Every citizen will also be allowed to designate the **party which is a second and/or third choice**, especially if the citizen suspects that the party of choice might not receive enough votes to enter Parliament. In this case, the second or third choice of party will be used as

the vote. This will enable new small parties to receive their fair share of the votes, so that voters will not have to worry that their vote might be wasted, if their first choice or even second choice do not cross the threshold.

5. Every citizen will receive a questionnaire which must be filled in and submitted to the electoral committee as a demonstration of each citizen's understanding of the party and candidate information received.

6. Every party will have to submit a balanced financial statement of its expenses on Election Day. Any breach of this regulation will disqualify the party from standing for election.

7. After the votes have been counted, the party with 51% or more of the electoral vote will have at least 61 members in Parliament and will be the majority party.

8. A party will enter Parliament if it secures 3.33%, that is, **four members** out of the 120 in Parliament **in the first vote**.

9. Parties with less than 3.33% of the electoral vote (four members of Parliament) will not enter Parliament. Votes for these unsuccessful parties will be transferred to the voter's second choice.

10. If no party receives 51% of the votes, there will be a second election. In the second election, only the two parties that received the highest number of votes in the first election will participate.

11. The winning party in the second election will have its percentage of votes increased to 51%, and consequently, will have 61 members in Parliament. All the other parties will have their number of parliamentary members reduced accordingly. The details of this calculation appear in Appendix 1.

12. The Parliament members from each party will be those who received the highest number of votes from the voters for their party. Each voter makes a list of the party members in order of preference. The electoral committee will do the calculation. If the voter for a particular party puts a candidate first, the candidate will get 120

points, the candidate in second place will get 119 points and so on. Then the electoral committee will count the votes received by each candidate for each party and the total number of points for each candidate will be calculated. The members of each party who will enter Parliament will be those who received the highest total number of points from their voters.

13. The newly elected Parliament will decide on the new annual budget.
14. Once the newly elected Parliament has decided on the new budget the candidates for ministerial positions will have to amend their plans accordingly.
15. The twelve government ministers will be appointed by Parliament from the committee's shortlist and will be required to implement the policies that will be legislated by Parliament. **They will not have the authority to make decisions on their own.**
16. Every second election (every ten years), the public will vote on the number of members that should be in the new Parliament. Voters will base their decisions on the proposed numbers of all the parties that will be sent to them. The number of Parliament members will be the average number proposed by all the voters.

Prime Minister

1. The head of the government will be the Prime Minister and that person will be the only head of state. The Prime Minister will be the leading member from the winning party that has a majority in Parliament.
2. The Prime Minister will **not** be elected by the other members of that person's party.
3. The Prime Minister will be the member of the winning party, who has received the highest number of points from the voters for that party in the parliamentary election. (See recommendation 3 in Election for Parliament.) Using this method, the most **popular** member of the winning party, as determined by the party's voters, will become the Prime Minister.

4. The Prime Minister cannot serve in this position for more than two terms in a lifetime. Having served two terms as Prime Minister, that person may serve one more term as a member of Parliament. Similarly, a person who has served one term as Prime Minister may serve two more terms in Parliament. No such person can ever serve more than three terms in total.

5. There will not be a deputy Prime Minister. In the event that the Prime Minister cannot carry out his or her duties, the member who was elected second in the ruling party will take the place.

Selection of Ministers by Parliament

1. After Parliament has decided on the annual budget, the candidates shortlisted for ministerial positions will amend their five-year plans to stay within the limits of the new budget, and then appear before Parliament to present their amended plan.

2. As discussed earlier, the newly elected parliament will interview the shortlisted candidates for ministerial positions submitted to them by the elected professional committee, and then decide who will be the twelve ministers. Members will vote according to their opinions and not according to the dictates of their party and will make the reasons for their choice public.

3. Subsequently, the elected ministers will have to submit annual progress reports to ensure compliance with their proposed plans.

The Workings of the Parliament and the Government

1. A vote of no-confidence in the government can take place no more than once every calendar year.

2. The Parliament can vote to dismiss a minister including the Prime Minister but no more than once in a calendar year with dismissal applying in two cases: a) When there is a 2/3 majority in Parliament for dismissal. b) When the public's rating of a Prime Minister drops below 50% in which instance a majority of 51% for dismissal will be sufficient. Party policy will not be allowed to dictate the member's vote. A new minister will be selected from the pool of candidates

selected by a committee before the previous election. If no suitable candidate is available, the committee for selecting ministers will have to submit a new list of suitable candidates for that position.

3. Any public servant, parliament member, minister or the Prime Minister, who is under criminal investigation or being prosecuted in a criminal court, will be suspended temporarily from his or her position in Parliament. The accused will be reinstated if found not guilty.

4. A truly democratic state cannot tolerate false information coming from its public servants. If the facts in a statement made by any minister, Parliament member, or any public official is in contradiction with the facts stated by any other public servant, both will be suspended and only one of them will be reinstated after being cleared.

5. Anyone, including public officials, who uses false information that caused the suspension of a public official will be sentenced to 10 years public works and lose their citizenship.

6. A Parliament member who is not satisfied with his or her party cannot switch parties. The only option would be to resign and be replaced by the next in line in his or her party according to the popular vote.

General

1. All Parliament members will receive a salary which is three times the median salary in the country. This total sum will include all benefits and cannot be changed.

2. Salaries of ministers, including all benefits, will be between 2-4 times the median salary in the country and will be decided by Parliament.

3. The Salary, including all benefits, of the Prime Minister will be four times the median salary in the country and cannot be changed.

4. The salary of all other public servants, excluding menial jobs, will not be less than the median salary, and no more than four times the median salary in the country.

5. There will be identical compulsory pension plans for all ministers, Parliament members, public servants and all other citizens.

6. Every Parliament member or minister must stop any involvement, direct or indirect in any other businesses.

7. For a period of five years after leaving office, a minister or Parliament member will not be allowed to work for, or be employed by, a company, or an owner of companies, which was affected directly by that official's decisions while in office.

8. Every citizen seeking a public service position must make public a detailed CV (see Chapter 30: *Application for Employment in a Public Office*) and comply with the requirements for a job in the public service.

9. Two independent computer centers run by public committees, supervised by all political parties, will be established for voting and polling purposes. A similar local computer center will be established in each area.

10. All votes will be sent to both these independent computer centers, and to the local computer center, in order to prevent vote tampering.

11. Two independent systems of transmitting information between citizens and the computer centers will be used. They will be independent of the computer centers.

12. Every citizen will be able to use a password to access the databases in the two computer centers and the local center, and therefore will be able to confirm that his or her vote has been registered correctly.

13. The election result will be deemed correct only when the registered vote, as tallied in both computer centers, is in agreement.

14. Any tampering with the parliamentary electoral system will be punished by a minimum of five years' public works.

15. All the activities of ministers, Parliament members, and all public servants, will be video recorded (including sound) and available to the public in real time. Three offices will be exempt from being immediately available online (see recommendation number 16.)

16. The activities of defense ministry, the foreign office and the Prime Minister's office will also be video recorded, but not immediately

available to the general public because of potential state security issues. However, activities from these three offices will be immediately available if they do not jeopardize state security. Other issues will be evaluated from time-to-time by a judge and become public, providing this will not affect national security. In general, all activities of every civil servant will be video recorded and kept on record. Not recording or erasing data can result in dismissal and prosecution.

17. Decisions concerning keeping certain activities secret from the public, and for what length of time, will be made by a judge.

18. Only issues of national security will be classified for predefined periods, the duration of which will be decided by a judge.

19. All ministers and Parliament members will have to clock their time, similar to every other employee in the country, and will have to publish their schedules online. They must have **all their activities** video recorded and open online to the public, except issues of national security that will be recorded, but not open to the public. All parliamentary activities, including committees, must also be video recorded and open to the public online.

20. Every Parliament member will have to vote on every bill (one of three options—yes, no or abstain) and make public any research and the consequent reasoning influencing the voting decision.

21. Citizens who supplied or are supplying religious services will not be allowed to submit their candidacy for any position in government, Parliament or any other public service position.

22. Religious leaders or suppliers of religious services will not be allowed to influence any citizen's vote in any way. Any violation will be punished by five years' public works.

23. In the public service, no concessions will be allowed for employees due to religious considerations.

24. Every public official, including ministers and parliament members, will have to sign an agreement stating that religious considerations will not influence their work in any way.

25. Any fraud or tampering with the democratic process will be punished by at least five years' public works and loss of citizenship.

Chapter 7

Legislature—(Passing New Laws)

The process of legislation in Parliament is, by its very nature, extremely complex. This process often panders to populist sentiments. However, even if the legislator has good intentions, a new law might achieve nothing, or worse, achieve the opposite results, if the law has not been researched and implemented properly.

It should be the duty of Parliament members to carry out proper research on all the aspects and considerations that should be taken into account in formatting every new law. They must get all the relevant input from all the parties involved and allow all their research as well as the proposed law to be open to scrutiny by their fellow parliamentary members and the general public. Subsequently, the legislator must follow up on the implementation and consequences of the new law and make all this information available to the public. The legislator must be personally accountable for the success or failure of his or her law (see recommendation 10 below.)

Obviously, in this short chapter, it will be impossible to cover all aspects of this complex process. However, I am putting forward essential recommendations to ensure that the legislative process will achieve its goals. These recommendations are designed to ensure that the legislator has the proper expertise and consults with experts. Furthermore, they will ensure that the legislator has done extensive research, that each bill and its wording have been properly scrutinized so that it can be easily understood by the average citizen.

The following are my enumerated recommendations for changes to the legislative system that, in my opinion, will remedy the existing shortcomings and make it more effective:

1. Every Parliament member must provide detailed justifications for proposed legislation.
2. Parliament members must prove to the public that they have the relevant qualifications to propose the law, and/or show the detailed CV's of the experts who are advising them.

3. Parliament members must show the public and other parliamentarians that extensive research has been carried out on every piece of legislation, report the time spent researching it, the information acquired, and the sources of information used for the proposed legislation.

4. Every proposed legislation must include details about the budget required, its sources, the schedule of budget allocation, and the **name** of the official responsible for transferring the budget to the relevant government departments.

5. Every proposed legislation must include the **name** of the person in charge of implementing the law, and the schedule for its implementation.

6. Every proposed legislation must state clearly that the Parliament members involved have no personal interest in the legislation and include explanations about the legislation.

7. The media, other Parliament members, the minister in charge of the relevant department, and the public will have 90 days to submit their comments. The legislator will be required to provide relevant responses to all these comments.

8. Every proposed legislation must be sent to a high school senior class, **to establish whether it can be understood by the average high school senior.** This will also serve as an important educational tool for high school pupils and will encourage them to get involved in the Parliamentary system in their country.

9. The final version of the law will be sent to another high school, where the pupils will read it, and answer questions to prove that the wording is simple enough for them to understand it completely. If they fail to understand it, the law will be reworded, and sent to another high school for the same evaluation.

10. Every new law must have the signature of the legislator who initiated it. That legislator will be held accountable if the law is not properly implemented and/or does not achieve the goals it was designed to achieve.

11. Every new law will also show the name and position of the official responsible for its implementation. That official will appear before Parliament and provide dates of future progress reports that will be submitted to Parliament and to the public.

12. The official responsible for transferring the budget will appear before Parliament and take personal responsibility for transferring the budget on schedule.

13. Every Parliament member <u>must</u> vote on every piece of legislation, either in person or remotely, and publish a justification for the vote and justify the time spent studying the new bill.

Chapter 8

The Comptroller General

The Comptroller General's duty is to act as a watchdog and periodically investigate all the activities of all government offices. This official submits reports detailing whether their duties have been executed successfully, and specifies what issues need to be addressed. The comptroller's function is extremely important because the goal is to ensure that the government functions efficiently and that it fulfills its duties in a cost-effective manner. Also, the Comptroller serves as a watchdog to uncover any evidence of corruption. However, at present, the fact that the Comptroller is appointed by the same politicians whose government offices that official is tasked with investigating creates the potential that pressure will be brought to not act with total impartially. Therefore, under present circumstances, it is unreasonable to expect that the Comptroller's reports will be written with total impartiality.

Israel is a perfect example of this lack of impartiality. The Comptroller General rarely, if ever, names the officials responsible for their offices' failings. Moreover, the Comptroller does not name the official responsible for correcting a particular office's failings. As a result, each new report criticizing the different government offices is alarmingly similar to each previous report. Consequently, the present Comptroller General's report has no effect on the efficiency of these government offices, and furthermore does nothing to address the issue of corruption.

The following are my enumerated recommendations for correcting the abovementioned shortcomings:

1. The Comptroller General will be appointed by a professional committee, whose members will be elected by the public every five years. The committee for selecting ministers can also be used for selecting the Comptroller General.
2. This committee, whose activities are available to the public online, will also publish and/or send all the CV's of the candidates for the

position of Comptroller General, to all the citizens for their perusal. (See Chapter 30: *Application for Employment in a Public Office*.)

3. In reports, the Comptroller General must name the managers and officials who have failed in their duties. Furthermore, the reports must specify whether these officials should merely be disciplined or dismissed from their duties.

4. The Comptroller General reports will be published and available to the public.

5. The Comptroller General must name the managers and officials responsible for implementing his or her recommendations, while also specifying the timeframe for the implementation of these changes. Any failure to comply with the report will result in the official responsible being summoned to appear before a Parliamentary disciplinary hearing.

6. If the same failures appear in two successive reports, the official responsible will be summoned again before a Parliamentary disciplinary hearing. If the responsible official fails to offer valid reasons for noncompliance at this hearing, that person will be dismissed from the relevant position and banned from ever again working in the public service. All these disciplinary hearings will be video recorded and put online, so that they are available to the public.

7. The Comptroller General will also publish the names of those public servants who did not cooperate with any investigation and their superiors will be obliged to discipline them.

8. Any information about suspected corrupt practices, uncovered by the Comptroller General, will be referred to the Separate Police Force and Prosecution Department for public servants for further investigation. (See Chapter 19: *A Separate Police Force and Prosecution Department*.)

Chapter 9

The Government's Legal Department

The Legal Department in every country today is part of the government. As a result, politicians are able to influence the election of judges, and sometimes even elect them directly. In the US, for example, the President appoints certain federal judges and influences the selection of judges serving on the Supreme Court. In addition, the government controls the Legal Department's budget, giving it leverage over the legal system. This is clearly in violation of an important basic principle of the democratic system, namely the separation between the three powers: the Executive, the Judiciary and the Parliament or Legislative Branch.

In my opinion, the Legal Department must be confined only to advising the government and Parliament on legal matters, and to giving legal services to the public. The Government's Legal Department should have no control or influence on the legal system! (See Chapter 17: *Courts and Judges-The Legal System.*)

The following are my enumerated recommendations:

1. The Legal Department will be headed by a minister who will be shortlisted by a professional committee, and then appointed by Parliament as described in Chapter 6: *Parliamentary System.*
2. The Legal Department will provide legal services to the government, Parliament and the general public.
3. The Legal Department will not be involved in selecting and/or appointing judges.
4. The Legal Department will not have any control, including budgetary control, over the legal system. (See Chapter 10: *The Legal Services Office.*)
5. The Legal Department will include the Legal Services Office (see Chapter 10.)

6. The Legal Department will draw up all the formats of contracts between companies and their clients, and between landlords and their tenants. **The use of these formats will be compulsory!**

The Legal Services Office

(See also Appendix 2)

One of the most important rights of a citizen in a democratic country is to be protected, both physically and legally. Obviously, we should be protected from criminals, but also from any abuse of power by the government, the rich and powerful, and large corporations. Most of us are under the illusion that lawyers are there to seek justice, and to protect us from all of these forces but in actual fact, these powerful forces use lawyers and the legal system to intimidate us.

I would like to illustrate how lawyers think. Go to any lawyer and tell him, "I have a contract with my friend/business associate, but now I realize that if I don't adhere to this contract, I can make another million. Can you help me?" What will this lawyer's answer be? The lawyer might say "This is immoral!" or maybe "You signed a contract and therefore you have a moral and legal obligation to adhere to it." But, no, his answer will be, "Give me a large deposit, and I will see what I can do for you."

At one time, if you wanted to dispose of your business partner, you would hire an assassin and risk being prosecuted for breaking the law. Today, if you have the money, you can hire a lawyer to destroy your business partner's life without risking any legal consequences.

If the above scenario seems far-fetched to you, my experience will prove the veracity of this phenomenon. In South Africa, I worked as a consultant to many companies, implementing ways of saving money on their electricity and water accounts. In return, I was paid a percentage of these savings. Most of my clients signed my contract, expecting me to save them relatively small amounts of money, and therefore agreed to relinquish a percentage of these savings to me. However, when I worked with big corporations, the savings were in the millions. When some of these large corporations realized that not only were the savings in the millions, but also that my fee was in the millions, they took advantage of the fact that I was a small business. Because of my small size, they knew I could not afford the litigation costs involved, and used lawyers who helped them to avoid paying what they owed me.

One such glaring personal example occurred when one particular large corporation, which owned many office buildings, signed my contract expecting me to save them money and, in fact, I saved them many millions. However, they did not pay me on time. When I complained to the manager, I was told, "Your payment is going through the bureaucratic process. Don't worry!"

Because the corporation continued dragging its feet, in desperation, I went to a lawyer who said, "Don't worry! They have to pay you because they have signed off on everything." After a year of waiting to be paid by this corporation, all the while incurring huge expenses, I went back to the lawyer whose response was, "Pay me a large deposit and I will see what I can do." In addition to nonpayment for my services, I lost even more money in legal fees and other costs, and, eventually, I was forced to give up because I could no longer afford the legal costs involved. Although I was the owner of a successful business, my company was too small to take on this rich, large corporation. As a result, my successful business was close to bankruptcy.

Overall, in 16 years, I lost 27 million Rands (half my income, which would be approximately 4.5 million in US dollars.) I also incurred legal and other expenses, due to non-payment of my fees by several large corporations. I could not afford the legal costs to receive justice, whereas they could afford the legal costs to avoid paying what they owed me.

A friend of mine also lost money for the same reason. You can find his story in Appendix 3.

All these cases against big corporations had the same scenario. Although their lawyers did not present any specific complaints about my work, they disputed everything, and put the onus on me to prove otherwise. I am sure that most of you know that you cannot take on a large corporation with deep pockets.

In desperation over these unfair situations, I would sometimes ask a lawyer, "Where is the justice here? Where is the morality here?" He would laugh in my face and reply, **"Justice and morality have nothing to do with the legal system."** What does this say about our unjust legal system?

Time and again, I have had to deal with lying, crooked, greedy lawyers, and have paid the price of this unjust system, that lawyers have created for their own benefit. Running a business with the constant fear of not being paid made me realize how widespread the shortcomings of our legal system are.

Today, if you are wronged, first you have to pay a lawyer just to move the process forward. Even if the lawyer does nothing, it will still cost you money. We live in a world where money determines who wins, but whether you win or lose in court, the only real winners are the lawyers. However, lawyers will convince you that **the existing legal system is the least of all evils**.

The problem with the legal system is not only confined to civil cases. In criminal cases, lawyers have convinced us that we must safeguard the rights of the accused, especially if the accused can pay well. But what about the rights of the victim? We are so busy protecting the rights of the accused that we have lost sight of the rights of the victim. It is time to balance the equation. For example, it is patently absurd that evidence against the accused, which was obtained illegally, is inadmissible in court. Why punish the victim for an honest mistake made by a third party?

Nowadays, some democratic countries are trying to address the issue of legal costs, by allowing a contingency system, whereby the client pays nothing upfront, and the lawyer is paid a percentage of the proceeds. But again, even these systems are built in such a way that the richer the party is, the better his or her chances are of winning. The movie "Erin Brockovich," starring Julia Roberts, illustrates the problem of a lawyer taking on a contingency case against a big corporation, which has unlimited funds to fight the case in court over a long period of time. In Appendix 4 you will find an example of my own bad experience with the contingency system.

Even if it is possible for you to find a lawyer who is willing to take your case on a contingency basis, you should understand that the lawyer is doing the work mainly for his or her own benefit. The lawyer's interest in the case might very well wane over time, especially if expected net income does not meet initial expectations. Moreover, if, down the line, the lawyer receives a more lucrative case, he or she might lose interest in your case, and leave you in the lurch paying the costs to the opposing party.

Similarly, it is common knowledge that in divorce cases, many lawyers promote adversity rather than conciliation, in order to make a fat profit from the difficult situation that married couples find themselves in.

The sad fact is that when your civil rights are violated, you need a lawyer whose services come with a high price tag. Similarly, if you are accused of a crime, you are burdened with huge legal costs, even if you are not guilty.

This loss of faith in the existing legal system is illustrated by the popularity of vigilante movies, where a person takes the law into his own hands and achieves justice through violence and other illegal methods.

Who wins with this system? Crooks, the rich, and obviously the lawyers.

Who loses with this system? The rest of us!

Why is the system so bad? How did it become so bad? Why are people in most democratic countries willing to put up with this situation? What is the solution, and how do we implement it?

I do not accept the concept that the existing legal system is the lesser of all evils. So, I am suggesting a different system which will work better. My system will ensure that everybody will be able to receive equal justice, regardless of one's financial situation.

Experience shows us that the best solutions are actually the simplest ones. The government that you elected should protect you. The state should provide you with legal protection through the establishment of a **Legal Services Office** that will provide exactly the same legal service to everyone, regardless of financial status.

We shall all be equal before the law, not only in theory but also in reality.

In the following section, I have made several numbered recommendations. My goals in making these recommendations are:

    a. To ensure that the public gets quality legal service at a reasonable cost. (See recommendations 1, 2, 3, 4, 10, 11, 12.)

    b. To ensure that justice is swift. (See recommendation 4.)

    c. To ensure that identical high quality legal services are provided for all citizens and companies, irrespective of their financial situation, and for all public servants, irrespective of their rank. (See recommendations 6, 7, 8, 9.)

   d. To ensure that innocent people do not bear any legal costs in civil cases, as well as in criminal cases. (See recommendation 14.)

   e. To ensure that only the guilty parties, either in criminal or civil cases, carry the burden of all costs to the state, to third parties involved, and especially to the victim. (See recommendation 24.)

   f. To ensure that all contracts between companies and their clients or their employees take both parties into consideration equally. (See recommendation 26.)

   g. To ensure that contracts between landlords and tenants give equal consideration to both parties. (See recommendation 26.)

   h. To ensure that the public has control over the quality of the legal service it receives. (See recommendations 10, 11, 27.)

   i. To ensure that lawyers do not have any financial interest in the outcome of court cases. (See recommendations 7, 8.)

The following are my enumerated recommendations:

1. **A Legal Services Office will be established. This office will be independent of the government or the legal system** (see Chapter 17), although the government will decide on its budget. This office will provide identical legal services to all citizens, irrespective of their financial situation, and similarly will provide services to all companies and public servants irrespective of their rank.

2. The head of the Legal Services Office will be elected by the public every five years, following the establishment of a new Parliament and government, and following the government's decision on the budget allocated for the Legal Services Office. Candidates will make their **detailed CV's** public. (See Chapter 30: *Application for Employment in a Public Office.*)

3. The voting public will receive the candidates' detailed CV's (see Chapter 30) as well as an assessment of the current manager, and relevant newspaper articles related to the operation of the Legal Services Office.

4. The candidates for the position of the manager of The Legal Services Office will submit their detailed plans for managing the Legal Services Office based on its annual budget for the next five years. Their plan will include their proposed methods for ensuring quality service to the public, and also commitments regarding **the expected average length of different court cases** in both the civil and the criminal courts.

5. The public will vote from home, exactly the same as for any other election.

6. Only the Legal Services Office will be allowed to give legal services to the general public or any organization.

7. Lawyers will be employed **by the state only**, either by the Legal Services Office or any other public service office.

8. **Lawyers will not be allowed to give private legal advice, work privately as legal consultants, or represent clients in court in a private capacity.**

9. All lawyers in the department will earn at least twice the median national salary.

10. This office, like every other government organization, will have an internet site. Every citizen who uses the services of the Legal Services Office will be required to rate, on scale of 1-10, the office and the lawyer whose services were used.

11. If the rating of a specific lawyer drops below 65%, that lawyer will be summoned for a hearing with the head of the Legal Services Office. If a lawyer is summoned for three hearings within a period of five years, his or her employment will automatically be terminated.

12. If the cumulative rating of the Legal Services Office drops below 65%, the head of the Legal Services Office will have to resign and a new department head will be elected by the public.

13. The operating costs of the office will be covered by the government budget and the fees for legal services. Penalties awarded to the state by judges will not be included in their budget, to prevent a conflict of interest.

14. **In both criminal and civil cases, <u>neither party will be charged up front for legal services</u> or for court costs. <u>Only after the verdict has been given, will the losing party pay penalties and cover all costs to the state.</u>**

15. How can the government finance this service? The answer is very simple. In every civil court case, once a verdict has been given, the judge will have to decide if both parties acted in good faith, in which case neither party will pay costs to the state. However, if the judge finds that one side went to court without a valid reason, that side will pay the full cost to the state as well as the costs to others involved in the case, such as all witnesses, including expert witnesses. In legitimate cases, in order to cover the costs to the state, the judge will impose extra financial penalties on the losing side, especially in the event of frivolous cases.

16. All meetings and activities of the Legal Services Office must be video recorded and open to the public, unless decided otherwise by a Supreme Court judge, who will make public his or her reasons for such a decision.

17. **<u>Meetings of lawyers with their clients will be video recorded, and will not be privileged</u>.**

18. There will be a branch of the Legal Services Office in every city.

19. The office will consist of different departments, such as the Criminal Department, the Business Department and so on.

20. The office will provide legal advice to the public through the telephone and all other electronic means. The client will be charged on an hourly basis, at the real cost to the office.

21. All information about judgments and settlements, as well as the length of court cases, will be made available to the public.

22. All other legal services will be at the real cost to the state.

23. People without sufficient means will be exempt from payment.

24. In criminal cases, the accused will be given a defense lawyer appointed by the Legal Services Office, and the state will cover all costs. If the accused is found guilty, all that person's assets, including gifts

to others and all other dubious tax shelters that should have been registered with the state, will be used to cover all the costs incurred by witnesses, by the police, or by the state, as well as to provide compensation for the victim or victims. Compensation for the victim or victims will be decided by the criminal court, and not dealt with separately in the civil court.

25. In cases against the government, when citizens feel that they did not receive satisfactory service, they have the right to approach the Separate Corruption-Police Force and Prosecutor's Office (see Chapter 19.)

26. The office will issue **compulsory contracts** to be used between companies and their clients, including insurance companies and banks, companies and their employees, and landlords and their tenants, which will give equal consideration to both parties. Any specific alterations to these contracts will also be done by the legal advisers in this office, while still giving equal consideration to both parties.

27. The head of the Legal Services Office will make an annual progress report available to the public. This will include all the details regarding the quality of the service given to the public.

Chapter 11

Commission of Inquiry

A commission of inquiry is sometimes appointed by the government to investigate serious incidents in the public service, the army or even in the private sector. However, a commission of inquiry that has been appointed by the government to investigate public servants or the government itself, obviously cannot be completely impartial, and rarely, if ever, will it put the blame on senior government officials, even if such a blame is clearly warranted. Therefore, if the government decides to appoint a commission of inquiry, or the public demands such an investigation, a separate body, independent of the government, should have the authority to appoint the members of this commission. This body will also define the goals and any limitations on the investigation.

The commission of inquiry will carry out its investigation without government interference but will be required to submit its recommendations to the government. These recommendations will be binding unless challenged in court, where the final decision will be made.

The following are my enumerated recommendations:

1. Whenever the need arises to appoint a commission of inquiry, whether due to a government decision or triggered by public demand, the head of the Separate Police Force and Prosecution Department for Public Servants will appoint the members of the commission of inquiry (see Chapter 19.)
2. The process of electing the members of this commission will be open to the public.
3. All the activities of the commission will be available to the public online. If this openness risks jeopardizing certain aspects of the investigation, the head of the Separate Police Force and Prosecution Department will allow these specific aspects to be kept secret for a limited period.

Chapter 12

Statistical Data Office

Statistical data is the tool that enables the government to operate and is the source of information that enables the public to evaluate the government's performance. As a result, the government has a keen interest in skewing the presentations in its favor.

It is well known that in non-democratic countries statistical data is unreliable. However, even in democratic countries, we must ensure that the statistical data are presented in an impartial and professional manner. Therefore, it is essential to establish a statistical data office that is independent of the government.

The following are my enumerated recommendations:

1. A Statistical Data Office should be established under the jurisdiction of the head of the legal system (see Chapter 17: *Courts and Judges—The Legal System.*)
2. The office will be tasked with communicating to the public all impartial statistical data about government activities and all aspects of society.
3. The office must have **free access** to all government and civil servants' offices. Limiting their access will be a criminal offence.

Chapter 13

Health Care System

An affordable national health care system is the norm in most democratic countries, with the US a glaring exception. Therefore, I do not see the need to justify this at length, since this system works well enough in most, if not all, democratic countries. Suffice it to say that it is unjust that a citizen without substantial financial means will be compelled to decide whether to buy food or save his or her life. My recommendations in this chapter are designed to improve the health service given to the citizens and to ensure that the health service will primarily concentrate on prevention of disease, and improvement of the quality of life of the citizens, rather than concentrating only on curing people after they become sick. However, obviously, the cost factor cannot be ignored. For example, if the health service has to spend one billion dollars which will only save a few people every year, a decision will have to be made about the most beneficial financial allocation in the health care service. In my proposals, the citizens will have a say in how the health budget is allocated.

The following are my enumerated recommendations:

1. The Ministry of Health will establish a department that will provide a compulsory health care system for all the citizens. This will include all medical costs, such as: medical tests, medications, hospitalization, <u>all</u> dental treatments and all treatments required for maintaining a good quality of life.
2. The Ministry of Health will deduct a fixed and equal monthly percentage, from all citizens' total income, for medical services. This percentage will be reviewed every five years, when a new government is appointed.
3. The balance of health costs will be subsidized by the government.
4. The Healthcare System will not only concentrate on curing disease, but rather will actively promote and subsidize services to improve the health of all citizens. These will include guidelines for healthy

living, consultations, preventive testing and free help for substance addiction.

5. All medical service providers, including pharmacies and hospitals, will be invited to participate in the health care system and negotiate a pricing system with the Ministry of Health.

6. Any citizen needing any type of medicine or medical service will be able to avail himself at every participating service provider or pharmacy of choice and will pay 5% of the cost. Expensive services like operations, hospitalizations and very expensive medications will be free of charge.

7. Once a year, the Ministry of Health will decide on the approved list of medications and operations. The Ministry of Health will send to all the citizens a list of medications and operations that it does not consider to be cost effective, together with explanations about the number of patients that will require them annually, and how treating these patients will affect the citizen's monthly payment. **Every citizen will vote for or against adding specific medications and operations to the approved list.** Those medications and operations that receive more than 51% of the vote will be included in the approved list and the monthly healthcare payment will increase accordingly.

8. Any person who is obese for no medical reason, or any person engaged in any activity, that puts individual health in jeopardy, such as smoking, drug abuse or alcoholism, will pay the state a higher monthly percentage of their income for medical insurance, in line with an expected, more-costly use of the medical system. Moreover, the deductible for these patients will be 15% instead of the normal 5%. This increase in the deductible will be a penalty for illnesses believed to be self-induced.

9. All medical service providers will be rated by the citizens who use their services. Medical service providers that receive an approval rating of less than 65% will be removed from the list of approved state service providers. Any service provider with an approval rating

higher than 90% will receive, for services provided, up to 30% more from the state.

10. All medical service providers will be required to ensure that every citizen is made aware of their rating before a citizen decides to use their services. All services with long term consequences will be rated annually by their users and these ratings will also be presented to all potential clients. For example, diet consultants will have to show their ratings given to them by current clients and the clients they had treated in the previous five years.

11. The medical services department of the Ministry of Health will also be rated by the citizens. If its approval rating drops below 65%, the General Manager will be replaced. If the General Manager has to be replaced a second time, the Minister of Health will resign, and the process of selecting a new Health Minister will commence as detailed in Chapter 6: Parliamentary System.

12. All citizens of retirement age will continue paying the same monthly percentage for medical Insurance from their pension and/or income. However, their contribution to the cost of services and medication will drop from 5% to 3%.

Chapter 14

Organ Donation

Nowadays there is no doubt about the importance of organ donation. However, in some countries, there is resistance to organ donation for religious reasons.

The following are my enumerated recommendations:

1. Organ donation after death should be made compulsory by law. However, the final decision will be at the professional discretion of the medical authorities.
2. Any attempt to prevent organ donation will be a criminal offense since it prevents the potential recipient from receiving lifesaving treatment.
3. The state should promote the understanding of the importance of organ donation.

Chapter 15

Defense Forces

The army is not managed like a business, which is required to make a profit, and is supervised by their auditors and shareholders. Furthermore, generals are not necessarily experts in managing their operations efficiently, and, as a result, might waste excessive amounts of money in the process of achieving their goals.

However, the details of defense operations in national defense forces are, by their very nature, confidential, and are not supervised financially by professionals as is the case in every private business. As a result, there might be a tendency for generals to ask for additional budget, instead of improving the efficiency of their operation.

The following are my enumerated recommendations:

1. A civil organization composed of economists and industrial engineers will be established to advise generals on how to improve the efficiency of their operation.
2. This organization will carry out inspections, and submit an annual report to Parliament, highlighting inefficiencies and wastage in the defense forces. This report should be made public.

Chapter 16

Gun Control for Countries with Free Gun Ownership

Free gun ownership exists in the US. There are historical reasons for this, but nowadays, free gun ownership is a result of the politicians' vulnerability to pressure groups like the gun lobby and gun manufacturers. This easy access to guns results in many deaths, and specifically the phenomenon of massacres by individuals. It also gives criminal groups, especially drug cartels in South America, easy access to guns that they purchase from American citizens. Furthermore, these guns might be used to undermine democracy.

The following are my enumerated recommendations for countries like the US where gun ownership is <u>not</u> forbidden or strictly regulated, and not for countries where gun ownership is forbidden already. I definitely do not promote gun ownership in countries where it is already forbidden:

1. Every weapon manufactured, imported, and/or sold in the country should have all its data, including ballistic data, recorded in a central police database.

2. Ownership of guns should be confined to 1-2 **hand-held non-automatic** weapons for self-defense, kept in a police-approved gun safe at the residence of the gun owner.

3. In addition to the above, ownership of guns should be allowed for certain recreational activities, like hunting and so forth, but should be strictly regulated.

4. Every citizen wishing to own a gun will be issued a certificate by the police if that citizen meets all the following conditions: (a) The citizen is 21 years old; (b) without a criminal record; (c) without a history of mental problems; (d) in possession of a certificate of

police-approved course in gun handling and safekeeping; and (e) in possession at one's residence of a police-approved gun safe which is equipped with an alarm system connected to a police station.

5. Buying or selling of guns will be allowed only to or from a police-approved gun shop and reported to the police. Individuals will not be allowed to sell guns to other people.

6. Gun shops will be regulated and periodically inspected by the police.

7. Every purchase of a gun will require a police certificate and all the details of the transaction will be reported to the police by the seller and the buyer.

8. When not in use, the guns will always be stored unloaded in a police-approved gun safe equipped with an alarm system connected to a police station, and never left out when the owner is not present.

9. The police should inspect periodically to insure that guns are safely stored.

10. No one should be allowed to carry a gun in public whether it is concealed or not.

11. Every gun owner must exercise the use of his or her gun at least once a year.

Chapter 17

Courts and Judges—
The Legal System

In theory, democratic countries are blessed with an independent legal system which brings justice for all. In practice, however, the legal system is far from being independent and it is clear to us all that justice is not always served.

The existing democratic system blocks the influence of politicians on court verdicts through the principle of separation of powers (parliamentary/ legislative, judiciary and executive powers.) This is an important cornerstone of the democratic system, whose purpose is also to ensure that no one will be able to gain dictatorial powers.

The legal department is part of the government. Therefore, its only duty should be to serve the government. However, at present, it also **controls the courts**, which violates this important basic principle of the democratic system, i.e., the separation between the executive and the judiciary systems. This violation enables politicians to influence the election of judges, and sometimes even to elect them directly. It is unacceptable that politicians are able to elect judges to the highest court in the US, and also have administrative and budgetary control over the legal system, as this gives them additional indirect influence over the court system.

The governmental legal department must be confined to serving the government but should not control the courts (see Chapter 9: *The Government's Legal Department*.)

It is my opinion that some democratic countries like the US and Israel have compromised the principle of the separation of powers, by allowing politicians to influence the judiciary system, either directly or indirectly, and, as a result, have compromised its effectiveness and its impartiality.

In this chapter and other related chapters, I am proposing changes that will guarantee the independence of the judiciary system. These changes will rectify many other existing shortcomings, like incorrect verdicts, the excessive length of court cases and their cost to the individual and the state. And, of equal importance, these changes will ensure that court cases do not impose sentences which are too lenient, something which is contrary to the intention of Parliament.

However, before I delve into the details of my proposed changes, I would like to share with you some of my personal experiences with the legal system, which highlight some of its shortcomings.

The following example was my first introduction to the sad reality which exists in the courtroom and also to the shortcomings of the legal system in general.

As a young boy, I used to believe that justice was a fact of life, and that the courts were the "Towers of Justice!" My childish notion was shattered when I was a young man. One day while I was driving my car, I started overtaking the two cars in front of me. By chance, there was a police officer in one of the two cars I was passing. This police officer wanted to pass at the same time, and he did so without looking in his rearview mirror and almost bumped into my car. As a result, he was startled, got upset, and fined me for overtaking dangerously. Since I knew that his accusation did not hold water, and because I had a hitchhiker in my car who had witnessed the whole incident, I decided to challenge him in court.

In court, both my witness and I described the incident truthfully to the judge. The police officer, who had no witness, presented his version of the incident, which completely contradicted the facts of the incident. The prosecutor emphasized the rank and reputation of the police officer, and without further deliberation, the judge found me guilty, and increased the fine. I was shocked! The judge had not only handed down the incorrect verdict, but he was also quite simply not interested in the facts of the case.

The indifferent attitude of the legal system to a witness can also be seen in Appendix 2, which illustrates another example of this phenomenon.

Later on in life, I paid dearly and repeatedly for the shortcomings of the legal system. I owned an Engineering Consulting firm in South Africa. Some of my corporate clients successfully used the legal system to avoid paying me a total of 27 million Rand, which I could not recover without getting myself into huge legal expenses that I could not afford.

I soon realized that I was not the only one in this difficult situation, as I had heard similar stories from many other people. In fact, several lawyers, those whom I hear lecturing about the legal system, have recommended avoiding the legal system as much as possible.

In this chapter (and other chapters), I am attempting to highlight the main shortcomings of the legal system. I am striving to remedy the existing unjust situation and make the courtroom a place of justice for all.

The first shortcoming that I would like to address is that the courtroom has become a playground for lawyers who have convinced us that certain tactics are necessary in order to protect the suspect from abuse by the state. In reality, the suspect's very expensive lawyer can invent all manner of fictitious scenarios that his or her imagination can come up with. This is what is called "a suspect's line of defense." A lawyer's job is to cast doubt on the suspect's guilt, leaving the onus on the state to prove the charge. The consequences of such a system are that, if you can afford the expense, you can hire a more proficient liar (in other words, devious lawyer) who will make it extremely difficult for the state to prove its case.

Therefore, in many cases, the state has no choice but to reach a settlement with the criminal that results in a reduced sentence, either because of the costs involved in a prolonged trial or because of the fear of "double jeopardy." The end result is that the criminal "gets away with murder" and receives a reduced sentence. **Is this justice?** What about the victim?

Furthermore, justice should be swift. Nowadays, police investigations and court cases often drag on for an unreasonable length of time, with the taxpayer and the suspect picking up the tab. This causes anguish to both the suspect and the victim.

The second shortcoming I would like to address is my belief that the **existing legal system does not provide the same protection for the poor as for the rich**. The richer you are, the better are your chances of evading justice, since you can hire a lawyer with better abilities to cloud the truth, which makes it less likely that justice will be done. In Chapter 10: *The Legal Services Office*, I have discussed how to remove the cost factor, and offer the opportunity for everyone, whether rich or poor, not only to get justice, but even more importantly, to get **equal justice**.

The third shortcoming is that laws are written with **incomprehensible** wording which cannot be understood by the average citizen. If we look at the laws in the Bible or the much earlier Hammurabi Laws, we can see how simple they are and how easily they could be understood by the average citizen. Even now, thousands of years later, it is easy for us to understand these ancient laws. Consequently, justice at that time was probably swifter than today. Nowadays, laws are written by Parliament members, some of whom are lawyers, with the assistance of other lawyers employed by the state, but without any input from the public about the wording. The result is that lawyers have a field day in interpreting these incomprehensible laws. Why did we agree to that? Lawyers have convinced us that they are protecting us from abuse of power by the state. But who is protecting us from the lawyers? The argument that the existing system is the lesser of all evils applies to the legal system as well as to the existing problematic democratic system.

We have discussed at length some of the shortcomings of the existing legal system. Now let's look at what we want from the ideal legal system. When we are wronged, we want immediate cost-free justice. When someone offends us, we want to be able to stop the offender immediately and receive compensation within days rather than years! This means that the suspect will no longer have any **excessive** rights, beyond the obvious rights needed to prevent injustice. The exercise of **excessive** rights, rights which are not necessary to prevent injustice, overtax the legal system with the extremely difficult, lengthy and costly process of establishing "burden of proof." The existing system often does not provide us with justice as was intended by the law and, as a result, justice is not being served. On the contrary, in many cases the guilty parties "get away with murder" or receive reduced sentences. We have to go back to basics! Justice cannot be slow, expensive and, as a result, inaccessible to many of us.

The following are my enumerated recommendations:

The Establishment of an Independent Legal System and the Status of Judges

1. The Head of the Independent Legal System will be elected by the public before the next Parliamentary election. The voting will be through the internet the same as any other election and voting choices will be based on the CV's of the candidates (see Chapter 30: *Application for Employment in a Public Office*) and other information that the voter will receive through the internet.

2. Candidates will make their detailed CV's public (see Chapter 30.) Any misinformation on the CV will be considered as fraud, and subsequently prosecuted, with a mandatory minimum sentence of five years' community service.

3. The candidates will submit their detailed plans for managing the department, including their choice of the administrative manager, as well as their **proposed annual budget for the next five years.**

4. All political parties will be required to make their views known to the voters on the **proposed budgets of the candidates** for the head of the Independent Legal System. When receiving this important and relevant information, the voter will be able to assess the merits of every candidate's proposed plan and budget.

5. The newly elected Parliament will be required to approve the budget of the newly elected head of the Independent Legal System.

6. Once the budget is approved, a new head and administrative manager of the Legal System will take up their positions.

7. The head of the Legal System will make an annual progress report available to the public.

8. All meetings and activities of the members of the Legal System must be video recorded, and available to the public.

9. A committee for selecting and appointing judges will be established by the head of the Legal System who will be its chairperson. The chairperson will have to confirm that committee members have no affiliation with any political parties. The whole process as well

as the CV's of the candidates will be put online and available to the public (see Chapter 30: *Application for Employment in a Public Office.*)

10. All judges, <u>with the exception of</u> high court judges, will be selected by the committee, which will be made up of half judges and half university law professors who are currently working in university law departments.

11. High court judges will be elected by a secret ballot of all judges and law professors in the country, and the results of this ballot will be published. All candidates for high court judges will have to make known to the public their world view, and, more importantly, their views on legal matters.

12. High court judges will only be allowed to serve for ten years beyond the mandatory retirement age. Moreover, their medical records should be accessible to the public. Their mental state should be evaluated periodically, and these evaluations should be made available to the public. In the event that there is any doubt about a judge's competence, the head of the Legal Department will appoint a committee of physicians to decide whether the judge is able to continue carrying out high court duties, and if not, the judge in question will resign.

13. All judges must earn **at least** twice the national median salary.

The Legal Process

1. When a crime occurs, the parties involved will be obliged to **answer all questions** put to them by the police and other officials and will be **obliged to tell the whole truth**. Not answering fully and truthfully will be considered a crime.

2. The judge will play an active role in finding the truth and will intervene in cases where there is a noticeable discrepancy between the skills of the lawyers involved. This is already the case in France.

3. In cases that require specialized skills which the judge does not have, like financial expertise etc., the judge will be required to appoint an expert who will also sit on the bench.

4. Clients' consultations with their lawyers must be video recorded, meaning that there is no longer any client/lawyer privilege.
5. The lawyer is not allowed to <u>invent</u> a "line of defense." The lawyer must present a line of defense which is based on the information told to the lawyer by the accused in a conversation which has been video recorded.
6. In civil cases, once a verdict is given, the judge will rule whether the case was reasonable or not. If the judge rules that the loser has not acted in good faith, that loser will be responsible for all the costs to the state, in addition to compensation for the victim and the victim's dependents.
7. The winner in a civil case will not incur any costs before, during or after the court case.
8. In criminal cases, the victim and/or the victim's dependents will be consulted and updated at every step of the process by all parties concerned, including the police, the prosecutor and the judge.
9. After conviction in the criminal court, the convicted criminal will be responsible for all the costs to the victim, the victim's dependents, the costs of the police investigation **and all other costs to the state**. The judge will give permission for the state to claim these costs from the convicted criminal's assets. The ruling on compensation to the victim will be decided immediately and not in a separate civil court.
10. If the police have a reasonable cause to suspect that the wellbeing of the victim or a witness might be in jeopardy, the judge can rule to put the perpetrators, or any known criminal elements related to them, like gang members, etc., into temporary custody, and supply the victim and/or witnesses with police protection, until the end of the trial.
11. If a witness or a victim of a crime dies of unnatural causes, his or her testimony will still be accepted by the court as true. This will remove any motivation to intimidate or harm these people.
12. Anyone summoned as a witness will be required by law to appear in court and tell **everything** known regarding the case. The state

will reimburse every witness for the costs incurred and any loss of income.

13. All tourists entering the country will submit their biometric data upon their first entry. This will help the police in their investigation to determine if the tourist is involved in any crime.

14. Tourists who have to appear in court, either as a victim or a witness, will be allowed to appear using video conferencing, even from their home country.

15. Everybody, regardless of their status or profession, must report to the police any suspicion or knowledge of a crime that has already been committed or that they believe might be committed in the future. No exemptions will be allowed for any status or profession, including residents, tourists, physicians, psychiatrists, social workers, lawyers or religious professionals of any kind.

16. All citizens and residents must appear in court if summoned and testify truthfully.

17. The prosecutor must consult with the victim before making the decision whether or not to proceed with the prosecution. Furthermore, the prosecutor must inform the victim of the reasons for each decision, which must then be published on the police internet site.

18. The convicted criminal will be solely responsible for all collateral damage caused by anyone else as a result of criminal actions.

19. The convicted criminal should never be allowed to take legal action against the crime victim or anyone else involved.

20. Citizens should be allowed to use any means to protect themselves or their property against an intruder, without having to consider the consequences to the attacker.

21. There should be no statute of limitations for any crime. If someone is found not guilty in a criminal case, that acquitted person can still be prosecuted again if new incriminating evidence comes to light.

22. All evidence acquired by the police or members of the public will be submitted and accepted by the court, irrespective of whether it was acquired legally or illegally.

23. Although members of the public or the police will not be allowed to acquire evidence illegally, if this evidence is acquired in good faith and in the belief that the action is necessary for the investigation, no prosecution will follow.

24. Any citizen who suspects that a judge is either incompetent or has ulterior motives can inform the head of the Legal Department, who will then be required to investigate the judge, take appropriate action, and publish the findings. However, if a citizen is not satisfied with the findings and subsequent actions, that citizen can file a complaint with the Corruption-Police Force and Prosecution. If this subsequent investigation turns up evidence that the judge is indeed incompetent or corrupt, the prosecutor will terminate the judge's employment and, if necessary, will submit the case to a trial by jury with the same jurisdiction as any other court of law.

Chapter 18

Police

The police force is an essential component of a democratic country since it is our only line of defense against chaos. Policemen risk their lives every day to protect us. They stand between us and violent criminals. They face violence on a daily basis, and, as a result, they work under a lot of stress.

In order to give you some insight into the **stress** that the policeman endures, I would like to share with you **four** personal experiences that I had while working as a volunteer policeman in South Africa.

On one occasion, my partner and I fought to protect some youths from a mob of drunken thugs who were beating these innocent youngsters senseless. Another time, on one particular dark night, I was checking for illegal activity in a park, when I heard shots and realized that they were aimed in my direction. On a third occasion I chased after a criminal who had shot a policeman. He ran away and led us on a dangerous high speed chase. When we finally cornered him, he put up his hands expecting to be treated humanely. He wasn't! Finally, to top it all, I felt devastated while attending the funeral of four police friends who had been killed in the line of duty.

From my 15 years' experience as a police volunteer in South Africa, I realize that there are four main issues that we should focus on:

1. The **stress** that the policeman endures.
2. The **financial temptations** that the policeman is exposed to.
3. The current **focus** on solving crimes rather than focusing on preventing them.
4. The **antagonism** that many members of the public harbor against the police.

Stress

First, the stress that the policeman experiences can cause that officer to use unnecessary force against innocent civilians. I do not have a magic solution for the mixed feelings that exist between the citizens and the police.

However, I do believe that we, the citizens, should **always** treat the policeman with respect and make that policeman feel appreciated. I believe that this will help to alleviate the issue of the use of unnecessary force by the policeman against civilians.

Financial Temptation

The second issue that is important to highlight is the temptation for the policeman to become corrupt and start taking bribes, or even worse, to co-operate with criminals. In many countries, the policemen do not earn enough to live on. In South Africa, I worked as a volunteer policeman with many regular policemen. I was shocked to learn that, during a 12-hour shift, they could not afford to buy fast food or even a cup of coffee. We, the volunteers, often purchased snacks for them. The low salaries earned by policemen in African countries, has resulted in the practice of taking bribes, as many tourists in Africa can confirm, since foreign tourists are an easy target for this corrupt practice. This is why we should make sure that our policemen are paid a living wage, so that they are not under constant financial pressure. This financial pressure can push them into breaking the law that they are appointed to uphold. On the other hand, all police activities should be carefully monitored. This can be achieved by equipping all policemen with video cameras which will record their activities while on duty.

Focus on Crime Prevention

Thirdly, there should be more emphasis on crime prevention. This has worked successfully in Japan and has substantially reduced the problems with organized crime there (the Yakuza crime organization.)

Public Antagonism

The fourth issue, namely, the antagonism that the general public has towards the police, is the most difficult to address. I believe that respectful behavior in encounters with the police should be a legal requirement. This will go a long way in reducing police aggression towards innocent civilians. Also, as mentioned earlier, equipping the policeman with body video cameras will improve relationships with the public, and will prevent the policeman from behaving inappropriately.

To sum up, my goal is to achieve a better understanding of the difficulties that a policeman faces and to specify our expectations of the police. I believe that crime can be substantially reduced if we implement the following recommendations:

1. A National Police Chief and Prosecutor will be elected by the public every five years. There will be no time limit for the number of terms that these officials are allowed to serve. All the candidates will submit detailed CV's (see Chapter 30: *Application for Employment in a Public Office.*) The candidates for Police Chief and Prosecutor will submit five-year business plans that will include specific goals, a timetable for achieving these goals and the required budgets. These officials will not take up their positions before their proposed budgets are approved by the newly elected Parliament.

2. There will be separate elections for the local Police Chief and Prosecutor in every city or county. They will be elected every five years by the people who they serve.

3. The elected National Police Chief and the elected Prosecutor will submit annual progress reports to the public.

4. **The main goal of the police will be crime prevention!** This will be achieved by assigning at least four policemen to every neighborhood, with at least one of them on patrol at all times. These policemen will have at least two years' post high school education, as well as special training in communicating and dealing with the general public. Their goal will be to become acquainted with the residents in the neighborhood that they serve. They will deal with all antisocial behaviors and activities and will be expected to predict potential criminal activity and, if possible, prevent it.

5. All the neighborhood residents will have the phone number of the policeman on duty.

6. All policemen will wear name tags and will be equipped with video and voice recording equipment, which will record and transmit all their activities to the police station throughout their shift.

7. **Every policeman will earn at least twice the national median salary!**
8. Every policeman will command respect from the public and will be addressed by rank or the title: "Officer."
9. Insulting or behaving disrespectfully towards a police officer will be an offence punishable by at least one day's community service in the neighborhood.
10. All policemen will have the power to punish anti-social behavior by issuing fines and/or by handing down a punishment of community service in the neighborhood for one day or more.
11. Members of the public will be required to rate the performance of every policeman they have had dealings with (see Chapter 28: *Feedback Organization*.) Any policeman, whose average rating drops below 65%, will be summoned to a disciplinary hearing. In high crime neighborhoods, public ratings of police officers will be evaluated carefully before summoning a policeman to a disciplinary hearing.
12. The public will rate the police periodically (see Chapter 28: Feedback Organization.) A National Police Chief and/or Prosecutor, whose approval rating drops below 65%, will be obliged to resign, and an election will be held for that position. The resignation will go into effect as soon as a new official is elected.
13. When a policeman conducts an investigation, everyone involved, including witnesses, will be required by law to answer fully and truthfully, and later to testify in court if summoned. Refusing to answer all questions fully will be considered a criminal offence.
14. The police and the prosecution, involved in a criminal investigation, will be required to keep the victim updated with frequent progress reports.
15. A policeman will be required by law to open a criminal file at the scene of the incident or the crime and will open an investigation: a) If the officer suspects that a crime has been committed, even if the victim does not wish to file a complaint; b) If the victim requests it; c) If a third party reports knowledge of a crime.

16. A criminal file will be opened on site, so that the victim will not be required to go to the police station in order to open a file.

17. All police and prosecutors' activities will be available to the public unless this information jeopardizes the ongoing investigation. This information must be made public as soon as it no longer jeopardizes the progress of the investigation.

The Obligations and Rights of the Suspect:

1. To answer truthfully and fully every question put by a police officer, prosecutor or that officer's legal representative, even at the scene of the crime.

2. To have the questions and answers video recorded both at the scene of the crime and subsequently at the police station.

3. To be represented by a lawyer from the Legal Services Office (see Chapter 10: *The Legal Services Office*.)

4. To have a legal representative present at all times, except during the initial questioning at the scene of the crime. This questioning will be required to be video recorded by a policeman.

I hope that my experiences and the above suggestions will contribute to a change of attitude of the public towards the police, and lead to a better relationship between the police and the public.

Chapter 19

A Separate Police Force and Prosecution Department for Public Servants

A major flaw in the existing policing system in democratic countries is that any investigation of public servants can be influenced or even controlled by the government. Therefore, such an investigation cannot be expected to be impartial. Even worse, expecting the police to investigate themselves with impartiality is nothing short of a travesty of justice. Furthermore, this lack of impartiality does not adhere to the democratic principle of separation of power. Although some might claim that opposition politicians will ensure that police investigations of public servants are impartial, in my opinion, such an expectation is unrealistic at best.

A real separation of power can only be achieved by establishing an Independent Police Force that will be responsible for investigating allegations against all public servants, including the police. This Independent Police Force will be completely independent of government control.

The following are my enumerated recommendations:

1. A Separate Police Force and Prosecution Department will be established to investigate allegations of corruption and/or criminal activity made against all public servants, including the police, all judges (including Supreme Court judges), government ministers, the Prime Minister and members of Parliament.

2. This Independent Police Force will also investigate information from whistleblowers in the public sector (see Chapter 37: Whistleblowers.)

3. **This force will <u>not</u> come under the jurisdiction of the government.**

4. This Separate Police Force will not be allowed to investigate itself. Any allegations against members of this force will be investigated by the regular police.

5. The head of the **Separate Police Force and Prosecution Department** will be elected by the public every five years.

6. All candidates will submit a detailed CV (see Chapter 30: *Application for Employment in a Public Office*.)

7. The candidates will submit five-year business plans, with their proposed budgets, goals, and timetable for the achievement of these goals.

8. All political parties will send the voting public their comments on the candidates' proposed budgets for this department.

9. The voting public will review the candidates' CV's, as well as their business plans and proposed budgets, and vote accordingly. It is important to note that voting for a specific candidate means acceptance of his or her proposed budget.

10. When a new Parliament is elected, it will be required to approve the budget of the elected Head of the Separate Police Force and Prosecution Department, who will then take up the position.

Chapter 20

The Penitentiary System

Nowadays, the penitentiary system is a huge financial burden on our society. In my opinion, the prison system should be used to generate income. The methods that will be used to generate income will be different for prisoners who do not pose a danger to society and those who do.

The following are my enumerated recommendations:

1. If possible, the court should always prefer to punish with public works rather than with prison sentence.
2. Anyone who receives a prison sentence but does not pose a threat to society or is not considered a flight risk, will reside in specially designated **open** and **unguarded** government housing.
3. The prisoners will be responsible for the maintenance of the facility.
4. Every morning the prisoner will go to work. The prisoner will work either in a previous job, or in a job which he or she was able to secure on their own. If the prisoner does not have a job, the state will arrange employment and pay a basic allowance.
5. The prisoner will usually work five days a week. However, if required, he or she can work extra hours. Prisoners who own a business will be allowed to choose their working hours. Prisoners will use public transport to go to work and return to their government housing immediately after work, **where they will be confined whenever they are not at work**.
6. Every prisoner will wear an electronic ankle bracelet.
7. The prisoners will be responsible for providing their own food.
8. Most of the prisoners' income will go to the state, which will allocate an appropriate amount to support their dependents, and a small amount will be retained by the prisoner for personal expenses.

9. Prisoners who violate their terms of imprisonment, and/or escape, will reimburse the state from their private properties or savings for the costs of recapture. Furthermore, that prisoner will be sentenced for additional jail time.

10. Violent criminals will be incarcerated and will have to work and finance the cost of their incarceration from their own income and assets that will be confiscated by the state. Alternatively, they will have to support themselves from the income they generate by working in government factories in prison.

11. Any prisoner who refuses to work will have much harsher conditions of confinement.

Chapter 21

Capital Punishment

There are crimes which threaten the individual and others that affect the general public. In contrast, there are also crimes that threaten society, the state, and the very existence of democracy.

The following is my recommendation:

Membership in a criminal organization, murder for hire and distributing illegal drugs should carry mandatory death sentence.

Our society must rid itself of such individuals since it is impossible to rehabilitate them. Therefore, the only punishment for these serious crimes should be mandatory capital punishment.

Chapter 22

Traffic Violations

Cars have changed the world for the better. Nowadays we are no longer confined to a small area of our residence, but we can travel all over the country and the world. With the blessing came the scourge of road accidents and car theft. To add insult to injury, we now have two wheelers that make our pavements a dangerous place to be. We can enlist modern technology to solve all these problems. With the use of modern technology, the state can save a lot of money on traffic policing, by enlisting the public to report traffic violations while they are happening.

The following are my enumerated recommendations:

1. Every vehicle will require a license, including those used by youngsters aged 13 years or older, be it, one-wheeler, two-wheeler, three-wheeler, or four-wheeler, cars or trucks used on the road or on the pavement. And each vehicle will be equipped with a GPS and cameras back and forth with a direct link to a police station.

2. The cameras will transmit visual data continuously and will have the option of transmitting vocal sounds. When the driver sees a traffic violation, he or she will press a button and report the details of the violation to the police center vocally.

3. Continuous video-recording from all types of vehicles will be activated when the driver ignites the engine without a key, or the vehicle starts moving. This will enable the police to catch vehicle thieves and also save a lot on legal expenses following road accidents.

4. To encourage the public and drivers to report traffic violations, the reporting public or the driver will be rewarded with 15% of the amount paid by the offending driver.

5. The police will be allowed to use the recordings to verify traffic violations, in particular **habitual offenders**. If the recordings are not sufficient to verify aggressive driving of these habitual offenders,

the police will station an unmarked police car next to the suspect's residence, in order to follow the suspect and record their driving offences. If the offending behavior is confirmed, the driver will lose their driving license for at least one year for the first offence, and for at least five years for the second offence.

6. The recordings will be used by the police and car insurance companies to verify reasons for road accidents.

Chapter 23

Issuing and Payment of Fines

I strongly believe that issuing **a fixed sum fine** for an offence is totally counterproductive. Today, the amount of the fine is related to the severity of the offence. This system does not take into consideration the fact that these fines impact different people in different ways, depending on their economic situation. In my opinion, in order for fines to be a deterrent, they should be related to the income of the offender. For example, a $100 fine for a supermarket cashier is a significant amount of money, but the same $100 fine is no deterrent for a millionaire. Even worse, a homeless person can be jailed for non-payment of a fine, which he or she clearly cannot afford to pay. Another serious issue is the increase of the sum of the fine as a punishment for non-payment. This is patently counterproductive, as this simply pushes poor people further into poverty.

The following are my enumerated recommendations:

1. All fines for any offence will be charged as a percentage of the offender's annual income, based on his or her previous year's tax return. Thus, a fine of 0.25% for a person earning $40,000 a year will only be $100, as compared to a fine of $10,000 for an individual with an annual income of $4 million.

2. An individual who does not have the financial means to pay a fine will not have that fine increased but will be assigned public work for the equivalent of the minimum wage until the fine has been paid off. For example, if the fine is $100 and the minimum wage is $20 per hour, the individual will be required to do public work for five hours.

3. If an offender's income has changed substantially since the end of the previous tax year, that offender can request that the government recalculate the fine based on his or her income in the last 12 months before the date of the offence.

Chapter 24

Labor Unions

Labor Unions were created with good intentions. They were created to curb the power that exploitative employers had over their defenseless employees.

However, the pendulum has swung too far in the other direction, as powerful National Labor Unions have become a self-serving force. In many instances, Labor Unions have become more powerful than the government, to the detriment of the country. There have even been cases where some trade unions have acted like criminal organizations, where racketeering has become endemic.

The many shortcomings of a national labor union can be demonstrated in Israel, a country which has gone from one extreme to the other. In the past, the Israeli Labor Union held excessive power and stifled efficiency and competitiveness in industry. Nowadays, the Israeli Labor Union, "The Histadrut" has lost its power, leaving most Israeli employees without any form of protection. However, there are still some remnants of the previous system in some monopolistic organizations like the ports, and the electricity company where management has little control over the employees who can close the ports or the electricity on a whim, to the detriment of the Israeli consumer.

I also had personal experiences with the Israeli National Labor Union, which demonstrate some of the shortcomings of this type of organization. The Israeli National Labor Union, "The Histadrut," is not as well-known as the British and American Labor Unions, but it is not much better.

In the following example, you will see how the Israeli Labor Union promotes itself in the eyes of the public, but when it comes to protecting the rights of its weakest employees, it shows no interest in their wellbeing, and, even worse, the union does not uphold the law and shows no concern for the national interest.

In 1971, the Israeli National Labor Union came up with a highly publicized program aimed at securing employment for problematic juveniles with criminal records. The union employed me, a 21-year-old youngster with only a high school education, to supervise a group of these kids in a small town, instead of employing qualified and more expensive social workers. The union organized employment for them, both in factories, and in the Israeli army. I succeeded in getting their cooperation and made sure that they went to work every day, which was my main task.

Some of the kids were employed in private industry, where they managed to acquire proper working habits. However, those who were employed by the Israeli army did not manage to acquire proper working habits, but the union never bothered to follow up on the failure or success of their program.

Gradually, I began to see cases of mistreatment of these kids by their employers. Mistreatment of employees by employers was not confined only to these kids, as this was how management routinely treated all their employees. However, instead of voicing their complaints in a legitimate fashion, or learning to accept their situation, the kids reacted violently to mistreatment. I convinced them not to react with violence, but to bring their grievances to me, so that I, as the representative of the Labor Union, could address these grievances.

When I brought their grievances to the Labor Union, I was ignored. When I insisted, I was fired! To make matters worse, I had to take the Labor Union to court to get the money that was due to me.

Years later, I was exposed to yet another glaring example of the union's self-serving attitude. I was working as a consulting Industrial Engineer in private industry in Israel. My job was to improve efficiency and establish work standards.

In order to encourage companies to improve efficiency, the Israeli government came up with an initiative that exempted premiums from income tax. These premiums are financial incentives for the workers to increase production. The workers were grudgingly willing to improve their efficiency in order to receive the tax exemption promised to them by the government.

I was hired by companies to establish work standards and I submitted reports to the management detailing work standards designed to improve efficiency. The management had to seek the approval of the National Labor

Union in order to adopt my recommendations. The National Labor Union put obstacles on my path at every opportunity. I realized that the union was only interested in keeping up the appearance of being concerned about their workers and to solve the problem I adopted the following solution. On my work standards' report, I did not add all the additional percentages due to the workers. This deliberate omission on my part could be easily detected. The union representative immediately noticed my "mistake" and gathered the work force for an urgent meeting, where he gave a long speech about employer exploitation. He claimed that the Labor Union had the employees' best interests at heart, and then pointed out my "mistake." I immediately "admitted" my guilt and added the missing percentage points. Then the union representative made a very passionate speech, stressing the crucial role the union plays in protecting employees. As a result, I was able to implement proper work standards, which I had been aiming for from the beginning and the union was able to keep up the appearance of taking care of employees' rights.

This worked more than once. I have no doubt that the union representatives understood what I was doing. However, they cooperated implicitly with me, since my "mistake" gave them the opportunity to conceal the fact they did not care about the workers.

Another example of the union's lack of morality can be seen in one of my meetings with them regarding my proposed work standards. The meeting was going badly, and I was feeling desperate, so I mentioned: "Did you realize that this is the Government's Efficiency Week?" Their reply was: "Maybe on the radio but not here!" This clearly showed the attitude of the union towards the government's initiative to improve efficiency in the factories.

The union and the employers put heavy pressure on Industrial Engineers like me to fabricate work standards that would enable the employees to get the tax exemption without actually improving efficiency. The unfortunate outcome of this practice was that most, if not all, Industrial Engineers like me, had to fabricate work standards in order to keep their jobs. As I was not willing to do so, I had to change my profession.

My proposals are based on the abolition of **National** Labor Unions. Instead, every employee will be protected by a **Local** Union.

The following are my enumerated recommendations:

1. National Labor Unions will be forbidden.
2. In every organization with more than 10 employees **the employer** will be legally obliged to ensure that a functioning Labor Union is established and operational in the organization. The job of this local Labor Union will be to bring employees' grievances to the management.
3. Every local Labor Union must act independently of all other Labor Unions. The local Union will not be allowed to join or cooperate with any other labor union or organization.
4. In any dispute between the employer and an employee, the employee can demand the presence of the union representative at every meeting with management.
5. The duties and activities of the union will be limited to dealing with employees' conditions and grievances against their employer.
6. The union will not be allowed to intervene in management policies and decisions.
7. The union will not be allowed to pressure the management on any issues which do not affect the employees directly.
8. If an employee has been working for three months consecutively on an hourly basis, whether as an employee or employed by a sub-contractor, the employer must change status so that he or she will become a monthly salaried employee of the company. This change of status will be calculated retroactively from inception.
9. All workers for the organization, including those employed by a sub-contractor, will be automatically protected by the local union from their first working day.
10. The Labor Union in every organization will be allowed to intervene in a dispute or strike only on issues related directly to the employees in the organization.

11. If the management genuinely has no control over disputed issues, like government decisions that affect the employees in the company, the Labor Union will not be allowed to call a strike. Moreover, the labor union in a company cannot declare a strike because of government policy, or a new law.

12. Before the Labor Union declares a strike, it must be able to prove that it has made substantial efforts to reach an agreement with management.

13. Labor Unions operating in monopolies and all government offices will not have the right to strike. They will settle their differences with the employer by bringing their grievances to arbitration or to the labor court.

Chapter 25

Office for the Protection of Employees' Rights

How do we protect employees from abuse by their employers? Nowadays, an employee can approach his or her union, or use prohibitively expensive legal advice. Therefore, in this chapter, I propose the establishment of an office for the protection of employees' rights.

In South Africa, an office for the protection of employees' rights has been established. However, this office is not run very professionally, since it does not employ experts in labor and employment laws, and, as a result, in every dispute the employer is forced to consult an expert at his or her own expense.

At this point, I would like to share with you how even such a well-intentioned step can fail in achieving all its objectives if it is not well managed, and why it is so important that the office manager's position depends on the evaluations of the employees using the office's services.

When I was running my own business in South Africa, an employee of mine approached the Office for The Protection of Employees' Rights with a complaint against my company that had no merit. Instead of employing professional consultants, the office sent the complaint to me, and I had to pay a labor lawyer to prove that the complaint had no merit.

Nevertheless, I believe that such an office, whose services are offered to employees free of charge, is essential, since it will ensure that every employee will have his or her rights protected. Furthermore, the employer will think twice before abusing employees, if he or she knows how easy it is for an employee to make a complaint against them. Employers will also be aware that they have not only to pay compensation, but also pay the office's costs and penalties. This office will also be extremely important since employees will no longer be afraid to become whistleblowers and come forward with damaging information about their employer. (See Chapter 37: *Whistleblowers.*)

The importance of this office is exemplified by the current situation in Israel. In more than 80 years of the country's existence, there have been very few whistleblowers in Government offices, and none at all in the private sector. Every one of these Israeli whistleblowers had his or her life destroyed, while the people they complained against were never prosecuted. The establishment of the Office for the Protection of Employees' Rights will surely encourage more employees to disclose illegal and immoral conduct in their organizations (see Chapter 37: *Whistleblowers*.)

The following are my enumerated recommendations:

1. An Office for the Protection of Employees' Rights will be established. The office will be under the jurisdiction of the elected head of the legal system, (see Chapter 17: *Courts and Judges –The Legal System*) who will appoint its general manager. Being under the jurisdiction of the legal system will ensure that the office will act with impartiality against any abuse of employees in the public sector.
2. The office will employ only professional and experienced labor law legal advisers.
3. There will be a branch of this office in every city. Employees will be able to come to the office in person or contact the office by phone or through the internet.
4. Every employee will be entitled to receive all the services of the office **free of charge**. These services will include legal advice regarding employees' rights in the workplace and handling grievances against their employer.
5. If an employee's grievance is found to be justified by the office's professional labor law legal advisers, they will approach the employer and take all necessary actions, including legal actions, until the matter is resolved.
6. In every case of justified complaint that was resolved by the office, the employer will pay costs and penalties. These costs and penalties will cover most of the office's operating costs.

7. One of the most important duties of the office will be to serve and protect whistleblowers. (See Chapter 37: *Whistleblowers*.)

8. The office will have an internet site, where every employee who has used its services will rate both the service received, and the professionalism of the legal consultant who handled a particular case. This information will also be forwarded to the "Feedback Organization" (see Chapter 28.) If the average rating of the office drops below 65%, the general manager will be replaced. If the average rating of a legal consultant drops below 65%, that consultant will be summoned to a disciplinary hearing.

Chapter 26

Employees' Salaries

In this chapter, I would like to introduce two concepts, one new and one old. The new concept that I propose is to impose a universal upper limit on employees' salaries. The old concept is the idea of giving a monthly bonus to all employees if the company has performed well. Unfortunately, this is currently not implemented universally.

An organization is a group effort so all employees should be remunerated according to a fair system.

I cannot see any objectively justifiable reason why the managing director and other senior employees are paid such huge salaries. We should remember that even an employee who is important to the company is just that, an employee, as even senior employees have not taken any financial risks. These risks are the prerogative of the owners and investors. Therefore, the managing director and senior employees should not be remunerated in a manner which suggests that they are solely responsible for the overall success of the organization.

There should be a compromise between the concept of equal salaries to all, an idea that has failed miserably, since it has stifled motivation, and the huge and unreasonable disparity between the salaries of the employees of most organizations under the capitalistic system. It is unreasonable and counterproductive to assume that some employees' contribution is so great that they deserve huge salaries, while the contribution of many other employees in the same organization is so small, that they deserve only a meager salary, which they can barely live on.

There should be a strict upper limit on employees' salaries.

I would like to share with you my personal experience that will illustrate my point, that even junior employees always make a substantial contribution to the success of the organization.

When I started working as an independent consultant in South Africa, my income from my clients was R17, 000 per month, so my annual income was R204, 000 (amounts which, in US dollars, are equivalent to $XX per month and $XX annually.) Later on, I realized that I could expand the business, but I could not do it alone because there was just so much that I could do on my own. Therefore, I employed a few people, all of whom had less than eight years of schooling. As a result, I was able to spend more time on actual consulting and not waste time on menial jobs, so the company's annual income rose to R1,800,000 (rose by a factor of 9) and my personal monthly income rose to R60,000 per month (rose by a factor of 3.5.) This example proves that even junior employees make a substantial contribution to the success of an organization, and that huge disparities between salaries are totally unjustified.

Before I introduce my proposal, we have to understand the difference between an average salary and a median salary. An average salary is the sum of all salaries divided by the number of salaries. A median salary literally means a salary that falls in the middle, meaning that, if you list all the salaries for every individual working in an organization in numerical order, the median salary falls in the middle of the list. Half the individuals on that list earn less than the median salary and half earn more.

I suggest a universal and compulsory upper limit for all employees' salaries set at four times the **median salary** of all employees in the country. However, in every **private organization**, the upper limit on salaries will be linked to the median salary in that organization **if it is higher** than in the country. Linking the upper limit on salaries in a private organization to the median salary in their own organization, will encourage management to increase the salaries of the lower half of their employees, since this will increase the median salary of the company, and therefore will be the only way that will enable them to increase their own salaries.

You might be wondering why I relate all the salaries to the median salary and not to the average salary. Calculating these limits based on the average salary is, in my opinion, not the correct way. The following example will illustrate the difference between an average and a median salary.

Let's say that we have a test group of five employees working for the same company. If one person earns a million US Dollars, and the other four in our test group earn 400, 300, 200 and 100 US Dollars respectively, the average income in this group is $200,200, while the median salary is $300. I believe that this example speaks for itself, as $200,200 is not a real representation of the income of members of this test group. High earners can use statistical averages to obscure the reality of unjustifiably low salaries.

If we assume that even the lowest paid employees can survive on their salaries, and that the median salary offers a reasonable standard of living, then my proposed upper limit of four times the median salary provides a very comfortable and rewarding, but not excessively high standard of living.

For example, the Forbes Advisor website reports that the median wage in 2019 in the US was $19.33 per hour, which translates into about **$40,000 per year** for a full-time job. Therefore, the annual income of salary earners in the US would be limited to **$160,000**. Nobody can argue that this proposal is based on Communist principles since the median living wage across the entire **U.S.** is only $67,690. The state with the lowest annual living wage is Mississippi, with $58,321, while the state with the highest living wage is Hawaii, with $136,437 per annum. Therefore, the majority of employees in the US, and all over the world, will not be affected by my proposed upper limit.

Just as every country has had to step in and legislate a minimum salary, every country should step in and legislate a maximum salary.

In conclusion, my proposed limit will affect only a small percentage of the employees in the country who earn unreasonably huge salaries. However, it will result in a more positive attitude of the employees towards the company.

My second proposal deals with motivating employees, so that they identify with the interests of the company. It is essential that every employee feels part of the organization. I used to tell my employees that I have no money to pay them. It is the client who pays them, so they should make sure to take good care of the client. This they did wholeheartedly because they understood the link between client satisfaction and company profitability and realized that their income depended on the level of our clients' satisfaction with our services. Furthermore, every month I paid them a fixed percentage of the company's income, provided that the company remained profitable. This translated to an extra 15% added to every employee's salary.

Similarly, I recommend that every company shares a percentage of its monthly profits among the workers which will in turn increase their motivation and commitment to the company's success.

The following are my enumerated recommendations:

1. The maximum salary in the country, including all benefits, should be limited to four times the median salary in the country. However, if the median salary in any private organization is higher than the median salary in the country, the highest salary in this particular organization will be four times the median salary including all benefits in this organization.

2. All <u>profitable</u> private organizations will give all their employees a monthly bonus of 15% of their monthly salary, conditional on the company's good performance. This will be in addition to the salary.

3. All policemen, teachers employed by the Government, Government ministers, judges and lawyers will earn at least twice the median salary in the country.

4. The salary of Parliament members will be fixed at three times the median salary in the country. This will encourage them to improve the salaries of low income workers and will prevent them from awarding themselves pay raises at their discretion.

5. The minimum salary in the country should be fixed as a percentage of the median salary.

6. Employees, including senior employees, will not be allowed to receive any additional bonuses, either while employed by the company or upon leaving the company, if this means that their total income will amount to more than four times the median salary as set out in previous recommendations.

7. The conditions of all citizens' compulsory pension funds will be identical. Their monthly contribution will be a percentage of their total income.

Chapter 27

Public Servants

The government and all public servants have a lot of power over us. This can easily lead to flagrant abuse of this power. In particular, the Internal Revenue Service's activities are open to abuse, and unfortunately can have a huge impact on the individual. Therefore, it is crucial that both the identity and all activities of public servants are available online for public scrutiny.

The following are my enumerated recommendations:

1. **Every public servant**, with the exception of only those applying for menial jobs, must be selected through a public tender, in other words through a public procurement process.
2. No politician or minister will be allowed to appoint anyone without public tender.
3. Political views of a candidate for a position as a public servant will never be a criterion in selecting him or her for public service.
4. Every public servant, except those doing menial jobs, will earn <u>at least</u> the national median salary.
5. Menial jobs like cleaners, guards, etc., who are not subject to a public tender, will earn at least the minimum national salary, and will be classified as government employees. They will be entitled to the same conditions as all other public servants.
6. Every candidate for a public servant's position must submit and publish a detailed CV. The candidate's CV will be published online. (See Chapter 30: Application for Employment in a Public Office.)
7. Detailed CV's of all public servants will be available to the public online, at all times.
8. The whole employment process must be available online, and the reasons for selecting or rejecting a particular candidate must also be published online.

9. The identity of the public servant responsible for any decision or action will be published online.
10. All public servants must wear a name tag with their name and position.
11. All public servants, including parliament members and ministers, must clock their working hours.
12. All government and public servants' activities will be put online and kept on record, with the exception of classified information pertaining to the Defense Department, Foreign Office and the Prime Minister's Office.
13. All government and Parliament meetings must be available online and kept on record, with the exception of the above mentioned offices (see recommendation 12.)
14. Anyone who has a criminal record or is under investigation for any type of crime will not be employed as a public servant.
15. Anyone who has lost in a civil court case, where the judge ruled that the accused did not act in good faith, will not be employed as a public servant. This will apply to both prospective candidates and currently employed public servants.
16. Any current or past provider of religious services will not be employed as a public servant.
17. Each government department will have a separate labor union. These separate unions will not be allowed to act in cooperation with the unions in other government departments.
18. Public servants will not be allowed to strike or take any organized action that will affect the functioning of any government office. Any such action will lead to prosecution, and the offending employees will pay full compensation for any disruption to government activities, or any damage done to government property.
19. Any public servant, who had the power over decisions that affected private organizations, either directly or indirectly, will not be allowed to be employed directly or indirectly by any such organization for a period of five years after leaving public service.

Recommendations regarding the Internal Revenue Service/ Income Tax Department:

20. All the activities of the Internal Revenue Service department will be available online, with the exception of ongoing investigations.

21. All income tax files of private individuals will be published online and made available to the public. The files of individuals whose income is less than four times the national median salary will be identified by a code known only to them. However, the files of high earners will have their names displayed at the top of their file in order to discourage any illicit deals with these high earners.

22. The tax files of all organizations and businesses will be published online with their names displayed for all to see.

23. Any decision of the Internal Revenue Service that appears in any tax file that does not strictly adhere to the letter of the law will have to be justified publicly.

Chapter 28

Feedback Organization

Feedback on services and organizations is not a new idea and it already exists in many forms. However, as it is not used universally at present, it does not serve as a sufficient deterrent, either to service providers who are able to get away with poor service, or to manufacturers who are able to sell deficient products to the public.

Although voluntary organizations, like the "Consumer Reports" publication in the US, already exist, the requested feedback from their readers is voluntary and does not apply to all products and services on the market. I believe that it is essential to make citizen feedback mandatory, so that it will become an important tool to be used by **all** citizens and applied to all products and services in the country.

For this tool to be effective, it must become the duty of every citizen to rate every private business and service. Furthermore, in order to improve the performance of our public servants, it should be mandatory for all citizens to rate the services they have received from them.

It must become the norm that, once you have used a business or a service, you must submit your rating for the service you have received. Although it might initially seem like a burden, with time it will become a habit, and when you start to appreciate the benefits of these evaluations, this "burden" will become a pleasure.

To avoid confusion, before enumerating my recommendations, it is important to clarify the different types of feedback:

    a. Immediate rating (1-10) when purchasing a product or receiving service from a private business or a public official (see recommendation 6.)

    b. At your discretion, you can add a description of your experience, any time after purchasing the product or receiving the service that you have already rated (see recommendation 4.)

c. Your response to a request for an annual rating of any product, like an appliance, that you have purchased.

d. Your response to a request for an annual rating of a service with long term effects like dietary consulting or physiotherapy etc. (see recommendations 11,12.)

e. Your response to a request for an annual rating of long term services, like your cellphone contract, cable TV, utilities, software or applications (see recommendation 12.)

f. Since all businesses and public servants will be evaluated by the public, the Feedback Organization cannot be a private organization, or be under the jurisdiction of a government office but must be independent of both (see recommendation 1, 2, 3.)

The following are my enumerated recommendations:

1. The Feedback Organization Office will be established to compile client feedback on every private organization, service provider, computer program and applications. This requirement for the public to give feedback will also include all public servants, including ministers, Parliament members, judges, lawyers and policemen.

2. The manager of the feedback organization will be elected by the public every five years based on the CV (see Chapter 30: *Application for Employment in a Public Office*) and work plan of the candidates.

3. The office will be under the jurisdiction of the independent and elected head of The Legal Services Office (see Chapter 10.) Since the office will not be under the jurisdiction of a government department, there will be no conflict of interest in the analysis and publication of the general public's feedback on public servants.

4. Every private business, every government office, and every cash register will be linked to the Feedback Organization to enable you to submit your rating easily and quickly. This rating will be as easy as punching in the code of your credit card at the cash register. Every client will rate the business or service on a scale of 1-10. Every business will have additional terminals for the clients to share, at their discretion, their experiences, at that business.

5. Every citizen will have a link in his or her cellphone to the Feedback Organization.
6. All citizens will be responsible for transmitting their rating of every business, public office, and/or public servant whose products they have purchased or whose services they have used. Moreover, if citizens wish, they can send a more detailed evaluation whether that evaluation is positive or negative.
7. Every private organization and public official will take down the details of every client and submit them to the Feedback Organization.
8. The names of clients and/or users of ongoing services like utilities, software and applications, will be transferred to the Feedback Organization on a monthly basis.
9. The Feedback Organization will compile the ratings and feedback received, and the general public will have access to this information.
10. Once a month, the Feedback Organization will send **every business and all public servants** their particular cumulative and compiled ratings over a period. Every organization and public servant will be required to display their rating and will ensure that it is easily visible for all to see.
11. The Feedback Organization will periodically send requests for evaluations to users of products with long term use, like appliances and cars, and services with long term consequences, like physiotherapists and dietary consultants. The Feedback Organization will then publish a statistical long term analysis of the ratings.
12. Once a year the Feedback Organization will send you a request to rate all the ongoing services and applications that you use.
13. Private businesses and public servants will be obliged to ensure that all their clients see their rating, including long term ratings, **before** the client decides to use a particular business.
14. The Feedback Organization will use their data to compile comparative statistical studies that will be sent periodically to all citizens, businesses and public officials in the country.

15. Every violation of this procedure by a business, public servant or a citizen, will result in warnings and if the warnings are ignored, they will face financial penalties.

16. Every **private business** whose rating drops below 66.6% will be assigned government observers that will publish their findings on a monthly basis. These reports will also be sent directly to the clients of each organization.

17. Every **private organization** whose rating drops below 33% will be closed by the government and its directors and owners will be forbidden from performing the same tasks again for a period of at least five years.

18. Every **public servant or public office** whose rating drops below 66% will be investigated by the comptroller general and the findings published. Furthermore, its manager will be required to rectify the faults within a predetermined period.

19. The **manager of every public office** whose rating drops below 33% will be dismissed and never work again for the government.

Chapter 29

Accountability of Public Service Officials

Recruitment for positions in the public service domain is a very problematic issue. In some countries, the President, the Prime Minister, and other ministers have too much discretion in choosing their subordinates, and often use clearly unethical considerations, like nepotism, when selecting a candidate.

Because these subordinates are unsuitable for their jobs, they, in turn, will use similar unethical considerations in the selection of their staff. Furthermore, new ministers are not easily able to terminate the employment of unqualified public servants when they come to office. Currently, the influence of citizens on the competence of public servants to do their jobs is, at best, marginal. Furthermore, unfortunately, public knowledge of how public servants are employed does not always deter ministers and other senior officials from employing unqualified staff.

In my proposals, I make it more difficult to employ unsuitable public servants by mandating full disclosure of the employment process to the public.

I want to share with you two personal stories which demonstrate and highlight this problem and its dire consequences.

The following first example is from my personal experience in private enterprise; however, it demonstrates exactly similar phenomena in the public service.

When I arrived in South Africa in 1991, I secured the position of Industrial Engineer in a large metal pipes factory. I was very successful in my work, and initiated several programs, including the use of computer-controlled production. To the young among you, I want to remind you that at the beginning of the nineties, computers were not used extensively like they are used today.

After a few months, the director in charge of the industrial engineering department informed me that I was being made redundant, because they had decided that the position of an Industrial Engineer in the factory was no longer necessary.

A year later, when I had established my own consulting business, I realized that I could expand it in various directions, so I called my previous Industrial Engineering manager to invite him to join me. He told me that the real reason why the director had dismissed me was because I was too good at my job and was too highly educated. Bottom line, the director feared the competition. Then my previous Industrial Engineering manager told me that, as a result of the director's decision to fire me, he himself resigned his position because he was disgusted with this unethical behavior.

The second example I have of this phenomenon, is from Israel. When I returned to live in Israel in 2006, I very quickly realized that putting my full qualifications on my CV for jobs that I was overqualified for, would guarantee that I would never be employed in my country. Therefore, on my job applications, I deleted most of my qualifications, leaving only my practical Industrial Engineer certification.

I saw an advert for a Practical Industrial Engineer in a government organization helping the blind. This government organization had established a factory whose purpose was to give blind people an opportunity to be gainfully employed. In addition, income from the factory was intended to supplement their social security payments.

I started working there and found myself working under a factory manager who was a retired Israeli army officer. He was honest enough to admit that he had no clue about management and was mismanaging the factory.

He was able to secure clients because the factory was doing the work for ridiculously low prices. However, at the same time, the blind workers were not getting 1,600 shekels a month as promised by the government but were getting only a few hundred shekels a month.

I immediately went to work, establishing proper paperwork and used cost accounting to decide on the price of the products.

Unfortunately, at some point I stupidly mentioned my true qualifications. The next morning, the managing director, who was also a retired officer with a fat pension from the army, called me to his office, and with usual

Israeli bluntness said, "We don't need university educated people here. Please leave immediately."

A few months later, it was reported in the media that the organization had gone bankrupt and was asking for financial help from the government.

In a democracy, it is important to give the citizens the power to terminate the employment of any public servant who is not suitable for his or her job.

The following are my enumerated recommendations:

1. All citizens who believe that a public official is not suitable for his or her job will submit a complaint. The basis for their complaint might be because they have received unsatisfactory service, or because they have substantiated knowledge of facts which, in their view, make that public official unsuitable for his or her job. If, in a citizen's opinion, a grievance is not addressed satisfactorily, that citizen can request a public referendum for the termination of employment of that official. The citizen can publish a complaint through the media and/or social media, citing facts that can be proven.

2. If the request for a referendum collects signatures from 10% of the electorate, the head of the corruption police will make an announcement requesting objections to the referendum within a period of three months.

3. If, after this three-month period, the number of supporters for the termination of this official's employment is larger than those who object, the state comptroller or the corruption police will conduct an investigation and publish the results of their inquiries.

4. The public official concerned will be required to tell his or her side of the story. This explanation will be sent to every citizen in the country who has the right to vote.

5. At this stage, the minister under whom this public official is employed will be required to set up a public hearing for that official. The minister will then decide whether or not to terminate the official's employment, and, whatever the outcome, the minister will publish a detailed explanation of the decision.

6. If the minister does not find sufficient cause to terminate the public official's employment, the state will send the relevant information to every citizen eligible to vote.
7. All citizens who are eligible to vote will participate and vote for or against the termination of employment of the official.
8. If the majority of the public votes to dismiss the official from his or her post, that official will be duly dismissed.
9. If the public official is a member of Parliament or a minister, a 2/3 majority in the public referendum will be required for that official to be dismissed.
10. Any citizen who calls for the termination of an official's employment using false information, will be sentenced to 30 days' community service and this wronged official will be allowed to sue for compensation.

Chapter 30

Application for Employment in a Public Office

You might wonder why I have dedicated a chapter to such a trivial matter like writing a curriculum vita (CV) or a resume. **In my opinion this is one of the most important chapters in this book.** As you will see, I require that the CV be detailed, and include failures! This transforms the CV into a tool for evaluating the performance of our public servants. For example, a Parliament member who will seek reelection after five years in office will have to detail his or her achievements and **failures**, and this will enable the voter to select the ones that actually spent the previous five years doing actual work for the citizens of the country and that their work had beneficial results.

There should be several requirements for application for any public office, be it ministerial, political, administrative or any other, with the exception of menial jobs.

The following are my enumerated recommendations:

1. Every citizen seeking a position in a public office, or any government office, must submit and make public a detailed CV, **including failures, in their previous positions**, financial statements, financial interests, and court cases the citizen was involved in. Furthermore, every position seeker must explain in the CV why he or she is qualified for the position they seek.

2. Every citizen, who was convicted in the criminal court, or lost a case in the civil court where the judge ruled that the citizen did not act in good faith, cannot serve in Parliament, or as a minister, or Prime Minister, or be employed in any position in the public service, or in the police force.

3. The CV must also include all information about the candidate's involvement in any religious institutions, past or present.

4. All applicants will submit a signed commitment that they will never use religious considerations in the performance of their duties.
5. Any intentional omission or misinformation on the CV will be considered as fraud, and subsequently prosecuted, with a mandatory minimum sentence of five years' community service. Any other omission will disqualify the candidate from public service.

Chapter 31

Education and the School System

Democratic values and the attitude towards equality and social justice must depend on the norms and morals of society, which are embedded in a youngster's mind from an early age. Therefore, it is naïve to expect that a society with non-democratic values would easily adopt democracy. In order to have a democratic country, we must ensure that the education of youngsters from an **early age** will rectify all non-democratic influences on them, whether these influences come from their parents and/or from their environment.

The separation of religion and state is a basic democratic principle. However, we see erosion in the separation between religion and state even in a democratic country like the US, which has adopted this principle in its constitution. For example, the US now has new laws against abortion that are religiously driven and clearly undemocratic. This indicates that, although many people are under the impression that American society is tolerant and democratic, there is a substantial part of this society whose way of thinking is religious, and if there is a conflict between religion and democracy, in their mind, religion wins. This, in my opinion, shows that the educational system has failed in raising a generation with democratic values.

We have seen the futility of trying to achieve major beneficial and democratic changes in a society that has been conditioned and educated with religious and non-democratic values, in the extremely religious Islamic countries in the Middle East. For example, in recent times, the US and the western powers brought the message of democracy to some Islamic countries in the Middle East, expecting to be embraced by the local population. This did not happen. Instead, they were greeted with suicide bombs, and none of these countries embraced democracy. On the contrary, all of these countries descended into chaos and bloody civil wars, so, eventually, the Western powers gave up and moved out, but only after thousands of their young soldiers, with a promising future, had sacrificed their lives needlessly. This was the result of the religious upbringing in these Islamic countries. This should be a good lesson for us, demonstrating the importance of **non-religious education** from **an early age**. This education will raise youngsters who embraced democratic values over their religious beliefs.

The importance of education for democracy from an **early age** could be seen when the Western powers forced South Africa to become democratic, and give voting rights to all non-white citizens, without going through a lengthy process of educating them to appreciate and adopt democratic principles. The result of this lack of education is that only a few non-whites today enjoy the benefits of democracy, usually because of nepotism, and certainly not because of their expertise. We also see how the South African economy has deteriorated and, furthermore, the country is now rated as a flawed democracy.

It is my goal in this chapter to make changes in the educational system that will counteract the religious and non-democratic influences that toddlers and youngsters are subjected to.

In this chapter, I introduce my recommendations intended to create a new generation that will grow up with democratic values, without being indoctrinated by religious beliefs, and will be ready and willing to become part of a truly democratic society.

The following are my enumerated recommendations:

General

1. A compulsory and cost-free educational system will be provided for all citizens' children between the ages of 3 and 18, including free transportation to and from school, all schoolbooks, computers, equipment, activities and school outings.
2. The school Principal will be responsible for maintaining a high standard of teaching, and for compliance with the requirements of the Department of Education.
3. A class should have a maximum of 20 pupils with two similarly-qualified teachers.

4. Education will be provided between 08:00-17:00 (that is, from 8 a.m. to 5 p.m.) five days a week.

5. School holidays will follow the same calendar as holidays established for all other employees in the country, except for three weeks' annual summer vacation, during which the state will provide organized, cost free, activities between 08:00-17:00.

6. All the activities and requirements of the Department of Education, as well as all school activities, guidelines, lessons and books, will be open to public scrutiny.

7. All classrooms in all the schools in the country will be equipped with online video and voice recording equipment, which will also be accessible in real time to all the parents of the pupils in that class.

8. Any parent who is dissatisfied with any aspect of his or her child's schooling can approach the Principal or the Department of Education with a complaint. The approached official must issue a response which deals with the complaint within two weeks.

9. Private schools will be allowed, provided that they comply fully with all the requirements of public schools.

Basic Educational Principles

1. All pupils will be introduced to critical thinking that is liberal, scientific, atheistic and independent, before religious dogma and other ideas that lead to prejudice have been implanted in their impressionable minds. This open-minded way of thinking is the backbone of any democratic country.

2. The concept of "winner and loser" must be replaced by the concept of "achieving the best you can be."

3. Teachers will have the freedom to choose how they teach, as long as they comply with the goals of the Department of Education.

4. There should not be any pressure on the pupils to achieve specific academic goals. Schooling should be fun for the pupils. Exams should be used as a tool to help them improve their knowledge and understanding.

Academic Staff

1. All the teachers must be well educated, have at least a master's degree in their subjects and be in possession of a teaching certificate.
2. Similar teaching qualifications should be mandatory for all teachers and assistants, whether for very young children or older teenagers.
3. All academic staff must accept that scientific thinking, questioning and logic are keystones of a civilized democratic society.
4. All academic staff must be well paid and earn at least twice the median national salary.
5. Academic staff should be allowed to use reasonable force to enforce discipline.
6. Teachers must command respect, and always be addressed by a title by the pupils and their parents. Mistreatment of a teacher by parents or any other family members will be punished by at least one day of community service. Pupils who behave disrespectfully towards a teacher will be severely punished.

Religion in School

1. Religions and the Bible will be taught in school from a scientific, atheistic, archeological and historical perspective, and its shortcomings will be emphasized.
2. The curriculum must include basic understanding and the history of most religions, with the emphasis on studying the Old Testament. The curriculum must also include clear explanations of how religions negatively impact the basic principles of democracy, in particular the negative effect that monotheistic religions had on the history of mankind.
3. The moral teachings of the Old Testament should be emphasized, as well as their relevance to our times. In addition, the shortcomings of the Bible's negative attitude towards non-believers should also be emphasized.
4. Religious practices must be banned from all schools.

5. No religious people or religious professionals, especially those who actively practice any religion, should be employed by the school in any capacity.

6. Parents who wish to provide their children with religious studies can do so at their own expense in private institutions, but only outside school hours.

7. Schools for religious studies will operate as private businesses and will have to register all donations as taxable income. They will not benefit from any subsidies or assistance from the government, private corporations, private persons or any other organizations.

The Qualities and Characteristics of a High School Graduate

All eighteen-year-olds, who are graduating from high school, should not only have acquired basic academic skills, but, more importantly, should also have acquired critical thinking skills, so that they are able to evaluate the choices that will be presented in their daily life, and are able to make informed choices concerning their duties to the democratic system in their country. High school graduates must have an understanding of the political process and must have a critical understanding and knowledge of all religions. To sum up, the graduate should have acquired all the skills necessary for a successful adult life in a democratic country.

The school curriculum must include:

1. **In-depth understanding of the democratic system.**
2. **Public speaking, debates, civics.**
3. **Knowledge and understanding of the relevance of history to our lives.**
4. **Philosophy, including the meaning of morality and the meaning of life.**
5. **Consideration and respect for all human beings.**
6. **Values: acceptance and tolerance of everybody, including the less fortunate in society.**
7. **Giving and accepting assistance.**

8. Pupils should be taught to treat the elderly with respect as part of the curriculum, so that they will understand that mistreatment of the elderly is immoral. Any mistreatment of the elderly should be punished.

9. Sex education, including the use of contraceptives, sexual orientation, and the definition of sexual harassment.

10. Marriage and relationships between married couples, and mutual problem solving.

11. Raising children and the effect on the marital relationship, and the expenses involved

12. Personal budget management.

13. Warnings against the use of dangerous substances like alcohol, cigarettes and illegal drugs.

14. Nutrition and healthy eating.

15. Memorization of songs from the Bible and poetry.

16. Writing good essays on different subjects.

Homework and exams:

17. Pupils should be given homework that requires an additional 1-2 hours of work at home every weekday, and more on weekends. This is so that they will get used to studying independently without direct supervision.

18. Exams should not be under any time pressure and with open books, so that they will not be required to memorize facts.

19. The use of multiple-choice exams should be discontinued.

20. Answers in exams should be mostly handwritten.

21. Children should be required to read specific books, write book reports and then discuss these books in the classroom.

Chapter 32

Religion

Religion and Democracy, by their very nature, are not compatible and cannot co-exist peacefully. In this chapter, I am proposing limits that a **democratic society must impose on religion**, in order to protect itself from being taken over. I am not naïve enough to expect that all of you will suddenly become atheists. However, in order to ensure that your children and grandchildren will also live in a democratic country, I am asking you to read this chapter with an open mind.

The Prophet Muhammad once declared that he was ordered to fight all men until they say: *There is no God but Allah!* With these final words, the Prophet summed up not only the vision of the faith he brought to the world, but also his own life story and political career. This philosophy is followed today by many Muslims, even by those who were forced to escape from their country because of religious persecution by their fellow Muslims. Despite this, they continue to follow their religious beliefs, and, more importantly, they try to enforce these beliefs on the Christian countries that have allowed them to live there peacefully, and with the right to practice their religion freely. This inability of many Muslim refugees to accept a new and liberal way of thinking endangers both themselves and others. This phenomenon is not only confined to Muslim refugees. The Christian pilgrims who escaped to America because of religious persecution, in turn enforced strict religious codes of behavior on their newly established society, causing much harm to many of their followers.

In fact, the first people to carry out a religiously-motivated extermination mission were the Jewish people. According to the Old Testament (Book of Joshua), they were commissioned by "GOD" to exterminate all the innocent pagan inhabitants of the "Promised Land," which they attempted to do with great enthusiasm.

Many years later, the Jews' strong religious beliefs resulted in much internal strife in the land of Israel, causing them to revolt time and again against various empires. These internal and external conflicts forced them into exile several times, the last of which lasted for more than 2,000 years. They had followed what they believed to be God's commandments, but God did not save them!

Similarly, the Christian religion cast Europe into the darkness of the Middle Ages for a thousand years. Religious control was strong in Europe until the advent of the industrial revolution which weakened the hold of the religious establishment in Europe. That is why many are able to live today in a democratic, tolerant and industrially advanced state.

It is true that life today is generally much better than in the past. This is due to advances in science and not due to God. However, even today, prosperity is not shared by everyone equally and life is still difficult for many. In contrast, it is ironic that in all three monotheistic religions, the priests, rabbis and imams live very well in our mortal world, while promising their followers paradise in their afterlife.

Nowadays, Christianity would appear to be the least problematic religion. Therefore, if you are a Christian, the changes proposed in this chapter might seem excessive to you. However, if you look carefully at the situation in seemingly liberal Christian countries today, you will see some disturbing religiously-motivated trends.

As a Christian, you will be free to continue to follow your beliefs and share them with your children. However, **at the same time**, you should **also** allow your children to be introduced to and understand liberal views that will be taught at school from an **early age**. This distinction is important because children almost always accept and follow their parents' beliefs, so once religion is planted in the minds of very young children, it is almost impossible to change their religious views.

The following recommendations are intended to gradually reduce the impact that religion has on future generations, and to prevent it from having a negative impact on all aspects of the democratic state.

The above points concerning religion have brought me to the firm conviction that **Monotheistic religions are the most dangerous enemies of Democracy**.

Now let's look at three recent examples of what religious professionals do when they are in power.

Firstly, let's look at the compelling example of modern Turkey. Ataturk, the founder of modern Turkey, was an atheist who established a robust democracy which enabled Turkey to prosper. However, unfortunately, a religious zealot by the name of Recep Tayyip Erdogan, has used the democratic process to be elected, and, subsequently, has used his power to drag Turkey backwards into totalitarian rule, in the name of Islam.

Secondly, Israel is another recent example of religious domination in a democratic country. The Jewish religious establishment has taken control of most aspects of life in Israel. Religion invades private homes and all residential and public buildings, including supermarkets, factories, farms, and even the Israeli military and the Israeli Parliament. In Israel, Parliament members and ministers who are religious, receive their instructions from their un-elected religious leaders. Incredibly, a Muslim Member of Parliament even declared freely in his inauguration speech that he receives his instructions from the Koran (the Muslim bible.)

Sadly, Israel has no constitution, and is the only democracy in the world without legal separation between state and religion, resulting in religious coercion in many aspects of life. The following are just a few examples of this phenomenon in Israel:

1. Religious courts control most marital issues.
2. Almost all food products grown, manufactured, imported and sold in the country must obtain extremely expensive religious certificates from different religious leaders, without which food producers and manufactures cannot sell their products in almost all food venues.
3. Most businesses are closed on the Jewish Sabbath and religious holidays.
4. There is no public transport on the Jewish Sabbath and religious holidays.
5. Free state burial is controlled by the religious establishment and reserved only for Jews.

6. The state employs tens-of-thousands of religious professionals who supervise most businesses in the country to make sure that they comply with religious laws. These religious professionals are not answerable to anyone, including even the government.
7. Every front door in every building and every internal door in every public building must have a Mezuza on the door post. The Mezuza is a religious object that must be purchased from a religious supplier.
8. Private businesses and state institutions are often forced to surrender to the demands of religious people.
9. Religious people in the street and religious employees at their workplace show their religious beliefs by wearing special clothing and demanding special food, even when they are employed by a secular organization.
10. Religious institutions exist in every neighborhood and are fully supported by taxpayers' money.
11. Religious service providers are exempt from tax.
12. All religious organizations are exempt from state supervision.
13. Religious practices of all kinds are conducted in the public domain, but do not have to be licensed by the state, unlike any other street vendor.
14. At taxpayers' expense, the Israeli army employs, and in many aspects is controlled by, religious people.

Thirdly, Iran is another recent example. Unlike Turkey and Israel, Iran used to be ruled by a totalitarian monarch who did not allow religion to dominate the country. At the same time, an Iranian religious leader was in exile in Europe and was very popular with the European media who did not understand how dangerous he was. In 1979, the Iranian people overthrew the monarchy, hoping that this would lead to a democratic government. However, once the revolution against totalitarian rule commenced, this religious leader came back, took power, and turned Iran into a totalitarian Islamic state that has become the main promoter of terror in the world, and has imposed intolerant religious laws on their own citizens and those of many other countries.

The best example of preventing the negative impact of religion on a state is Singapore, which practices complete separation between religion and state. As a result, all religions there coexist peacefully, and do not have any impact on political life. However, I have to confess that this is not a perfect example of religious coexistence in a democratic state, because Singapore, in spite of all its benefits, is not a democratic state.

My goal is to keep religion as a private matter and eliminate its negative impact on the government, on the legislature, on our public life, and on our cost of living. Most importantly, we should eliminate, or at least substantially reduce, the influence of religion on the younger generation.

The following are my enumerated recommendations:

1. The constitution will include complete separation between religion and state (see Chapter 4: *The Constitution*.)
2. No religious professional will be allowed to affect the voting of citizens in any way.
3. No religious courts will be allowed! All citizens will use the state court system.
4. Any organization wishing to provide religious education to youngsters can do so as a private business, outside school hours, i.e., 8 a.m. to 5 p.m. five days a week, during school vacations, and during the three-week annual school summer vacation.
5. Anyone who practices a monotheistic religion will not be allowed to work in the public or private, non-religious, school system, with the exception of religious schools which will operate outside public school hours (see Chapter 31: Education and the School System.)
6. No religious professional, present or past, will be employed by the state, or hold any public office, or be consulted by any public official or government employee or representative.
7. All candidates for public office will have to sign a commitment stating that their religious beliefs will not be a consideration in performing their duties, and that they will not consult a religious practitioner on issues related to their duties while they are in public

office. Furthermore, candidates will not demand or be granted any extra consideration at work because of their religious practices.

8. Private businesses and state institutions will not be allowed to give special consideration to the specific needs of religious people stemming from their religious beliefs.

9. Religious organizations, institutions and religious service providers will not be allowed to advertise their services publicly.

10. Citizens will be allowed to practice their religion only at home or on the premises of a religious organization which is officially registered as a business.

11. No one will be allowed to identify, demonstrate, or display his or her religious beliefs in public in any manner, including specific clothing, ornaments, jewelry, hair style, beard, or any other way, that identifies them as believers of a religion.

12. Religious people or institutions will not be allowed to perform any religious actions in the public domain, including prayers, sirens, bell ringing, or calling their believers to prayer through loudspeakers.

13. All religious institutions, like churches and mosques, will be registered as businesses, and therefore will pay tax on all their income, including donations.

14. Any citizen who wishes to provide religious services must register these services as a company, and therefore will pay taxes on all income, including donations, in the same way as any other private organization.

15. The state will not be allowed to subsidize religious organizations under any circumstances.

16. The state will be prohibited from giving any exemptions to religious organizations, meaning that they will be treated in the same way as any other private organization.

You probably feel that such limitations on religious people are excessive, especially if you are a Christian in a democratic country. But let me remind you again that Christianity plunged Europe into the Dark Ages that lasted for 1,000 years. And, without my proposed changes, history could very well repeat itself. Moreover, if you are a protestant descendent of the Pilgrim Fathers in the US, your ancestors might well have been fugitives from religious persecution by the Catholic Church in Europe.

As you can see, my proposals are not designed to prevent a religious person from practicing his or her religion, but only to prevent someone from having a negative impact on the lives of secular people in the public domain and on the democratic state.

Chapter 33

News Media

It is no news to anyone, that a free and independent news media is a critical cornerstone of democracy. However, it is clear to everyone that the essence of free speech in the media has been compromised, when we see that President Donald Trump can call the tycoon who controls Fox News directly to make various demands, or that the Israeli Prime Minister Bibi Netanyahu is supported shamelessly by a tycoon, who publishes a free of charge "newspaper" whose sole purpose is to promote him.

It is my goal to ensure that every citizen will get daily news from at least one reliable news media source. The public will get news from organizations that are not profit driven. Advertisers and politicians will not have influence on the media.

Every reporter will be reasonably qualified, properly remunerated and without other financial interests that might affect that reporter's journalistic work.

The following are my enumerated recommendations:

1. Freedom of the press must be in the country's constitution.
2. All news media organizations: newspapers, radio stations, TV stations and news through the internet, must be registered as nonprofit organizations.
3. In order to prevent excessive control by one media organization, each news media nonprofit organization will be allowed to use only two Media channels out of the four (newspapers, radio, TV and internet.)
4. All news media organizations must be completely independent of each other.
5. All news media will not be free of charge. The government will decide on the minimum cost of a news outlet for the public. For

example, the government will decide on the minimum cost of a newspaper that will be related to the actual cost of publication.

6. If there is no technical way to charge for the news service through the radio or any other channel of communication, then news will not be transmitted through this channel.

7. Every citizen will be obliged to subscribe to at least one newspaper.

8. **Only registered news media organizations will be allowed to report news.** No other private or public organizations will be allowed to report news!

9. Private organizations or individuals will be allowed to publish commercials that will have the name of the organization or individual that submitted it, and the price that was paid for it.

10. Every news media organization will be allowed to accept commercials from one individual or organization for up to 3% of its total advertising income.

11. If advertising is made conditional on positive news coverage, this will be considered as a crime against democracy, punishable by a minimum five-year jail sentence. Acceptance of such an arrangement will be similarly punished.

12. Any pressure by politicians, members of the public, private or public organizations, or any tycoons, to influence the media, will be considered a crime against democracy, punishable by a minimum five-year jail sentence.

13. Every employee of a media organization will be required by law to report to the police and the public any attempt at influence by a politician or that politician's subordinates.

14. Owners of multiple businesses will be required by law to ensure that all the organizations under their control will not contribute more than 3% of the advertising budget of one media organization.

15. The government, or any other public servant, will have to submit the same information to all media sources in the country, will have to invite all of them to every media briefing, and will be forbidden by law to favor one media source over another.

16. It will be a criminal offence for any politician or that politician's subordinate to contact only one media organization directly or indirectly.

17. A strict code of conduct will be enforced on all media organizations and reporters. Infringements will be considered a criminal offence punishable by at least a one-year jail sentence.

18. All editors and journalists dealing with news and information to the public will earn at least twice the median salary in the country. They will have to make public any income or financial interest they have from any other sources.

19. Every media editor or news journalist will have to make public a detailed CV (see Chapter 30: *Application for Employment in a Public Office.*)

20. Publishing fake news will be a criminal offence, punishable by, at least, a five-year jail sentence.

21. The tax returns of every news media nonprofit organization will be available to the organization's subscribers and the public.

22. Every news reporter will have to make his or her tax return available to the public.

23. The code of conduct for reporters must be strictly enforced by a reporter's committee and the government.

Chapter 34

"Fake News" Online

One of the ills that affect all democratic countries is the widespread phenomena of fake news through the social media, like Facebook and others, that can't be distinguished from real news. The problem is especially acute during election time and sometimes has major impacts on the election process. Recently, during the Covid epidemic, when governments made major efforts to vaccinate their populations, the social media was full of fake news pretending to promote legitimate professional opinions or research which "proved" the toxicity of the vaccinations and the negative effect on people that are vaccinated. This had a major effect on the willingness of the public to be vaccinated, prolonged the epidemic period, and caused many millions of unnecessary deaths.

One idea that might alleviate the serious problem of fake news on social media is to compel internet companies to ensure that every message on every social media channel will show the name of the original publisher, date of first publication, and the country of origin of the message.

As a result, every fake news item, which has been transferred many times by unsuspecting recipients, will always show the identity of the source, so that it can be evaluated by the recipient, and, if necessary, the original writer can be prosecuted by the authorities.

Chapter 35

Marriage, Divorce and Having Children

The situation today is that marriage and having children is considered as a God given right. As a result, people get married and have children without being prepared for the role of a spouse and a parent. Many people are not ready for the challenges of married life, which may lead to misery and ultimately divorce. Even worse, most young adults do not have the skills and knowledge of how to raise children. Although most people in democratic countries think that this is simply a private matter, when the family unit disintegrates, the state's social services are often required to step in and as a result we all end up carrying the financial burden.

The institution of marriage should be taken very seriously. In my opinion, the state should take reasonable steps to ensure that the institution of marriage is not entered into lightly. Even more importantly, the state should ensure that potential parents understand that having children must be given serious consideration, not only because of the effect on their young lives, but also because of the subsequent negative impact on their adult lives.

Every baby should have the right to be raised by mature parents. Those parents should have a reasonably good marriage. They should understand their duties to each other and to the newborn. Furthermore, they must know how to raise their child and must have the necessary financial means to raise him or her.

The following are my enumerated recommendations:

Marriage and Divorce

1. In order to be granted a marriage license, the couple must both be over the age of 18 years. They will be required to undergo pre-marital counseling with a social worker appointed by the state. This will

ensure that they both understand the seriousness of the step that they are about to take.

2. Once the social worker has ascertained that the couple understands the difficulties, and is mature enough to take this step, they will be allowed to get married.

3. A couple who wishes to get divorced must attempt to solve their problems with the help of state-run counseling sessions followed by a cooling off period of one year.

Having children

1. No one under the age of 18 should be allowed to give birth.

2. A pregnancy under the age of 18 should be terminated.

3. If the pregnancy of an underage girl cannot be terminated, the child will be given up for adoption, so that the teenager can grow up without the burden of an unplanned child, who she is not capable of raising.

4. An unmarried woman over the age of 18, who becomes pregnant, will be obliged to terminate the pregnancy or give the child up for adoption, unless she finds a partner and gets married.

5. A child born to an unmarried woman will be given up for adoption, unless she gets married within a reasonable period of time.

6. Giving birth will be allowed only if the state has issued a license. This license will be issued only to a couple. Single women or men will not be allowed to raise a child.

7. An unplanned pregnancy will be allowed to continue only if a marriage license has been issued.

8. Married couples who wish to have a child will be required to attend a state-run course, which will include the basics of raising a child, so that they understand the child's physical and emotional needs.

9. After this course, the couple will be required to have a consultation with a social worker. The social worker will assess whether the couple are mature enough to raise a child, understand the responsibilities involved, and have sufficient financial means to raise a child. Only then will the state issue a license allowing them to have a child.

10. If a sexual encounter results in an unplanned pregnancy, the man will not be held accountable against his will. However, if the pregnancy is terminated, the male partner will pay half the cost of the termination.
11. A single woman or man will not be eligible for a license for raising a child, even if there is another person who is willing to take financial responsibility for the child, unless they are willing to get married and form a family unit.
12. If the state can produce sufficient evidence to prove that a marriage license was issued fraudulently, in order to enable a woman to become a single mother, the couple will be prosecuted. And, if it is deemed to be in the child's best interests, the child will be given up for adoption.

Chapter 36

Private Organizations

There is no doubt that the European and American economic success was largely due to the invention of the concept of "limited liability" that enabled entrepreneurs to take risks and have the freedom to initiate and expand new commercial ventures without risking personal financial ruin. However, banks nowadays infringe on this principle of limited liability by requiring many entrepreneurs to sign private liability for loans to start a business. On the other hand, companies that fall on difficult times or close down, very often, use this privilege to withhold payments due to their employees.

While we definitely benefit from this free market system in the western world, the question is whether economic success is divided reasonably between all members of society, or whether there is only a small minority who reap most of the benefits. In the US, for example, there had been a realization that this minority of excessively powerful tycoons is a major problem and an obstacle to the economic progress of the American nation. US President Theodore Roosevelt (served 1901-1909) and some presidents after him, realized the need to curtail the power of individual tycoons. They used the Sherman Act of 1890, an anti-trust law which was passed for this purpose, as well as other anti-trust legislation, to break up large corporations, thereby enabling economic progress.

There is no doubt that the western world prospered due to private enterprise. However, the citizens benefited from their success to a large extent due to government control over their activities.

Nowadays, we can see this phenomenon of excessively powerful large corporations in many western countries, including the strongest economy in the world, the USA. For example, it is no secret that the powerful tobacco industry has been accused of adding nicotine to its cigarettes, resulting in many deaths from lung cancer etc., meaning it has literally got away with murder. In fact, governments are afraid to pass legislation to limit tobacco companies' harmful activities due to potential exorbitant legal costs, since the tobacco industry uses their financial resources to challenge governments in court, in order to prevent such laws. Similarly, Monsanto was accused of causing death and destruction worldwide, especially to farmers in the Third World, and of using their financial power in the US to intimidate farmers who dared to challenge them. Therefore, society needs to be wary of these wealthy large organizations, because we cannot deny that money is power, especially in our existing legal system.

The above examples lead us to the understanding that the existence of excessively powerful private organizations can result in at least five consequences that are detrimental to our democracy and our society. First, they can dominate the government. Second, their power enables them to dominate the free market and restrict competition. A third point is that they can use their power to cause harm to their consumers and even the environment. Fourth, large corporations can use their financial power to dominate the media and use false information to influence public opinion. The fifth issue is the impact that large corporations have on society's attitude towards corruption (see my personal story.)

Therefore, I have come to the conclusion that excessively large organizations endanger both the democratic system and the capitalistic system of free competition. We should have better methods for supervising the activities of all private businesses and particularly large corporations whose size should be limited and consequently give the general public a larger share of the economic prosperity in their own country.

Before we delve into my enumerated recommendations, I would like to share with you some experiences I had with large corporations in Israel, that demonstrate the fifth issue (see above), illustrating the underhand way that large private enterprises endanger democracy, on the one hand, and the important role that government can have in curtailing that power, on the other hand.

A few years after returning to Israel in 2006, I heard of a much-advertised initiative by a large cellular corporation to employ some elderly staff in their call center. In a company employing thousands of very young employees in their call centers, they decided to employ 25 elderly staff, and I was one of the "lucky" ones. We had a course that lasted a few weeks, passed an introductory exam, and started working.

I had always complained about the devious ways that companies in Israel treat their clients. Not surprisingly, after only one day, I was made aware of the company's policy to deliberately cheat their innocent clients. Our job was to deal with clients' complaints, knowing full well that they were being cheated. One member of our elderly group immediately protested, "You cheat clients, so I don't want to be a part of this," and then he resigned. I admired him! But as I needed the job, I could not make myself follow his example.

We were rated on one thing only: how fast we were able to terminate the telephone conversation with the client. If a conversation lasted more than a few minutes, we found the supervisor breathing down our neck, and standing impatiently by our side. I immediately and consistently found myself in conflict with my supervisors because I tried to solve the clients' many problems. Worse than that, we were expected to accept a new call immediately even though we had to make the corrections requested by the previous client. I was reprimanded repeatedly for spending the time making the requested corrections between calls. The youngsters avoided being reprimanded by making the corrections while listening to the complaints of the next client. As a result, the youngsters made a lot of mistakes, and the clients couldn't understand why their requested corrections were not always fulfilled properly.

We quickly learned the real policy of the company: "The Company does not compensate the clients fully, unless it receives a lawyer's letter." Since only a small percentage of clients were willing to risk paying for legal expenses, the Company was able to get away with fully compensating only these few clients out of all the clients who complained about being overcharged.

Almost all of our managers were youngsters. These twenty-one-year-old managers used to preach to me, "Adam! You don't have the Company spirit! The Company spirit means taking care of the Company, and not the client!"

Another incident that highlighted this Company's attitude towards its clients occurred when a client asked me to check which package was the most beneficial for him, as his family had a total of five cellphones. Why did he need my help? Because at the time, Israeli cellphone companies used to offer their clients various packages, but intentionally made it extremely difficult to choose the cheapest and the most suitable one. So, it took me twenty minutes to retrieve the information from three different computer systems that were not totally compatible, and sometimes gave contradictory information. After two hours, my supervisor appeared next to me and asked me why I had not received any phone calls for so long. When I told her what I had been doing, she looked at each phone number and immediately gave me the answer that I should give the client. I replied that I had checked, and that she was mistaken regarding some of the phone numbers. Her answer was: "So what?"

At one point, I sent an email to the managing director detailing the short-comings of the system and my suggestions to rectify the situation. I received a standard dismissive letter. After seven months, the company finally dismissed me. By then, only three or four elderly employees were left out of the initial 25 in our group.

That is when I realized why all Israeli companies prefer to employ the very young and not the elderly. Older people are not so inclined to cheat clients, while younger people have no empathy with the customers. They simply did what they were told.

Why am I telling you this? Because once employees internalize corruption, it permeates through to society at large. Corruption becomes accepted as the norm, and as a result it affects people's ability to recognize and condemn corruption in other spheres of life, including in politics.

The story of the Israeli cellular phone industry does not end here. A few years later, the Treasury Minister implemented a policy that broke the cartel of the cellular companies, allowing free competition. Prices of their services immediately dropped dramatically, and the company where I had been working, as well as all the other cellular companies, were forced to implement all the policies that I had suggested previously to my managing director.

The political aspect of this story is that this Treasury Minister, since then has been dubbed the "Social Minister." However, this was his only success, ever!

This demonstrates the important role that a responsible and professional government can have in reducing the disparity of power between consumers and all private corporations, especially large corporations.

In fact, the Israeli cellular industry is a perfect example of the negative effect that large corporations can have on the economy and society and this example highlights the importance of government involvement.

Before I leave the subject of my cellular phone company experience, I must report that a "miracle" happened! My previous managing director at the cellular company, the one to whom I had complained, was dismissed from his job. This was the only time I had ever heard about a managing director in Israel being dismissed for failing in his job. But you don't have to worry about him. He walked out with millions of shekels that could easily support many of us for the rest of our lives. This is money that came out of the pockets of Israeli consumers, who had been overcharged for cellular services for years.

The effect that employers have on the morality of their employees and consequently on the society at large, can also be seen in the following personal experience that I had while working as a cashier in a supermarket.

I used to advise clients if they unknowingly took food products that were damaged or had passed their expiry date. Also, I would point out if they hadn't noticed a sale price which could save them money, as well as directing them to other bargains that could work to their advantage.

When the managers noticed what I was doing, they instructed me to stop talking with the clients. When I did not obey these instructions, I was fired. After I was fired, I had a conversation with other cashiers who, like me, were earning a minimum wage of $7-8 per hour, in a country where the cost of living was far higher than in the US. They said, "Adam, why do you care about the clients? You need the job."

Another pressing problem with the way private organizations conduct themselves in our modern world is the way the new high tech industry works. Although this industry has brought huge benefits to our society, it comes with many drawbacks. Most if not all software and hardware products are not designed to be user friendly in two very critical aspects. Firstly, they do not take human engineering into consideration, and secondly, if upgrades are needed, they are inevitably very expensive. Also, most software nowadays is complicated, and if the customer has problems using it, the companies are quick to blame the customer for his or her ignorance. Therefore, I believe that we must impose better human engineering practices on the high tech industry (see recommendation 31) and furthermore, the high tech Industry should be treated the same as other engineering areas. For example, when a building is finished, the architect and/or the designer must take full legal responsibility for any future problem. When a bridge is constructed, the engineer must also take full legal responsibility. Software and hardware products should have the same certification.

In Appendix 6, you will find an example that demonstrates the lack of consideration for human engineering in the last few decades.

Before I enumerate my recommendations for this chapter, I want you to recognize that my goals are to:

    a. Prevent corporations from becoming so large that they are powerful enough to intimidate and dominate the government (recommendations 1-3.)

    b. Ensure that companies do not withhold information that is important to their consumers, to the public and to the government (recommendations 4-10.)

    c. Ensure that the original purpose of the protective status of proprietary (Pty) limited companies will be upheld. They will be confined to protecting the company from its creditors and will not protect its directors from being held responsible for their employees, their consumers, and the government if the company fails. Even if the company has closed down, the directors will still be responsible for actions for which any other citizen would be held legally liable (recommendations 11-13.)

    d. Prevent international companies from using tax shelters to avoid paying taxes (recommendation 14.)

    e. Prevent international companies from using their status to make it almost impossible for their clients to take legal action against them (recommendation 15.)

    f. Minimize shady practices of companies which harm their consumers (recommendations 16-24.)

    g. Ensure that all high-tech products are consumer friendly (recommendations 25-26.)

Having stated my goals, I make these enumerated recommendations:

1. Very large private organizations that exceed either the value of $1 billion or 1% of the annual government budget should be forbidden from purchasing or gaining control of other companies. However, they will be allowed to invest in other companies, but will not be allowed to have any involvement or control over them.

2. Any organization which controls more than 33% of its market share will be defined as a monopoly and will be forbidden from purchasing any company which is in competition with it.

3. Every existing large organization which **currently** exceeds 10% of the annual national budget should be required to sell some of its assets, so that they do not exceed 1% of the annual national budget (see recommendation 1.)

4. The Government will appoint government employed **internal observers** in every large and/or monopolistic organization. The internal observers will be government employees. However, every individual organization will pay the government for the cost of its observers. Similarly, internal observers will be appointed in smaller organizations that are suspected of shady practices that can adversely impact their consumers. The internal observer will stay in one company no more than two years, and subsequently, that observer will be replaced by another one.

5. Internal observers will have access to all company meetings, activities and files. They will be bound to secrecy, like all company employees, on issues that do not impact the general public or the government.

6. Government appointed internal observers will publish monthly reports for the public and the government. They will report to the government on **every illegal activity** in the organization. Also, the observers will report to the government, with a copy to the organization, whenever the company withholds **information, which might affect the public detrimentally**. This information will enable the government to further implement policies to protect the public.

7. Companies that wish to replace their **financial auditors** will have to show the government a valid reason why they wish to do so. This will prevent company pressure on their financial auditors to moderate their reports in order to keep their jobs.

8. Every large organization will have all its management and directors' meetings video recorded. All documents and video recordings will be kept for at least 30 years, even if the company has closed down.

9. **A "<u>Government Customer Protection Agency</u>" will be established. One of its duties will be to regulate the information that suppliers will have to make available to its customers and the form in which it will be displayed.**

10. Private organizations will be required to publish <u>all</u> information on their products or activities that <u>potentially</u> have an adverse effect on their customers.

11. Private organizations will also be required to publish <u>all</u> information that might have adverse effects on the general public or the environment.

12. The directors of every organization will be held criminally liable for not disclosing information on any of their products or activities that are potentially harmful to their customers, the general public, or the environment. Similarly, they will be held criminally responsible for every illegal act of the company. They will continue to be personally liable for actions during their time in office, even if they no longer work for the company or if the company has closed down.

13. If the government imposes financial penalties on a company, the company directors **will always** be prosecuted because financial penalties alone are not a sufficient deterrent to a large company.

14. Company Directors will be legally responsible for fulfilling their obligations to their employees, even if the company is in financial difficulties or even after it has closed down. The company must have sufficient reserves and/or proper insurance to guarantee that their employees will not be affected by the company's financial difficulties, or if the company closes down, irrespective of the reason.

Specifically, company directors will continue to be held personally responsible for fulfilling their employees' rights, even if the company has closed down.

15. Every international company should pay income tax in the country where the income has been generated, instead of paying tax in the country where the company is registered.

16. The legal jurisdiction for disputes between an international company and its customers must be in the customer's city and country of residence.

17. An ongoing contract between a company and its customer can be for a maximum of 12 months. The contract cannot be automatically renewed without the signature of the client.

18. All contracts between companies and its clients and/or employees must be issued only by the government.

19. Customers who have an ongoing contract with a company must receive a monthly letter and an email with a link that enables them to cancel the contract easily.

20. When a customer is overcharged, that customer must be reimbursed, with interest, from the original date, and penalties from the date of complaint. If there is a delay in refunding the money, the company must add daily interest until the full sum has been received by the customer.

21. Any delay in reimbursing the client will be considered a criminal offence and the company director responsible will be prosecuted.

22. Every business that sells to the public will not be allowed to change the prices of its products or services within a period of three months. However, it can offer its products at sale price only once during this three-month period and then sell the products again at their original price.

23. Industries like the travel industry whose products have a specific date, i.e., date of flight or date for occupying a hotel, will be allowed to reduce the price at their will until the due date. They will not be allowed to increase it again before that date. Furthermore, if the

price of the same product (i.e., an airline flight) is different through another source, the official price at the time must also appear.

24. Every company will have to disclose the planned life span of its products. Nowadays, most electronic and electrical appliances are purposely built to have a limited life span. The customer must be made aware of this fact.

25. All food shops, food vendors and supermarkets will have to display clearly any relevant and potentially harmful information about its food products, including health risks. This information will be on the shelf, and on the shop's internet site. The way the information is displayed, and its content will be standardized according to the regulations of the aforementioned "Government Customer Protection Agency."

26. Food products that are packaged by the shop, or sold by weight in bulk, must have their source, supplier, purchase price to the vendor, picking date, storage, etc. posted next to the product and in a format approved by the Government Customer Protection Agency.

27. Every shop selling any kind of item, including food products (whether it is a market, supermarket, etc.) must show the date of purchase, the identity of the shop's supplier, and the price that the shop paid for the item which will be posted next to the product.

28. Every shop or vendor which sells food, like fruit and vegetables, must show the name of the supplier, the price that was paid for the food item, date of picking, and any adverse information and complaints known to the shop or vendor. The format and contents of the sign must be approved by the Government Customer Protection Agency.

29. Every software and/or hardware product, which is sold to the public or to businesses, must be certified by an industrial engineer who is an expert in human engineering.

30. Every software and/or hardware product must be upgradeable, with the cost of the upgrades stated clearly. These upgrades should not be exorbitantly expensive.

31. Every private business whose rating by its clients drops below 33% will be closed by the government. Its owners and directors will not get similar license for a period of five years.

32. **It is in the interest of the public to prevent the creation of dynasties.** To prevent the creation of tycoon families, inheritance taxes will be at 75%, including all gifts given to others, provided that the amount left will enable all living descendants to retain the lifestyle to which they had been accustomed. The Government will ensure that no tax shelters will be available.

Chapter 37

Whistleblowers

The sad reality is that most of a company's corrupt activities are not carried out by the company directors, rather they are carried out by the employees who are forced to commit corrupt acts by those same directors. Therefore, we can understand the important role that whistleblowers can play in curtailing the power of management in fostering corrupt and illegal activities.

It is well known that employees with information about illegal activities in their corporation who approach the police or the media, or try to take legal action against their employer, very often have their lives destroyed.

One of the most important duties of my suggested Office for the Protection of Employees' Rights (see Chapter 25) will be to protect **whistleblowers**.

The act of **whistleblowing** is an extremely powerful tool which ensures that detrimental information about a company's or government's actions will become public. It is in the public's interest to ensure that every employee with detrimental information about his or her company's activities, or possessing such information about a government office, will not be intimidated, and will approach the authorities with critical information.

The protection of whistleblowers will reduce the ability of private organizations and public officials to circumvent the law by intimidating their employees.

The following are my enumerated recommendations:

1. Every employee in the private sector that has detrimental information about his or her company's activities, be it illegal actions or actions that might have adverse effects on the public, can walk into the: **"Office for the Protection of Employee's Rights"** (see Chapter 25) and be granted the status of a whistleblower. Similarly, every public servant can approach the **"Separate Corruption Police Force and Prosecution"** (see Chapter 19) and also be granted the status of a whistleblower.

a. The whistleblower's details and the details of the complaint will be withheld, at the whistleblower's discretion; until charges are submitted, or until the government takes any other action against the employer, like appointing observers.

b. If no legal action is taken against the employer, the details of the whistleblower will be withheld at the whistleblower's discretion.

c. If legal action is taken, the rights of a whistleblower will include continuing his or her salary by the employer until a judgment is given.

d. If the employer is found guilty, that employer will pay compensations to the whistleblower and will be responsible for maintaining the whistleblower's income until his or her retirement, either as company employee or working elsewhere, at the whistleblower's discretion. If the information is found to be false, the whistleblower will have to reimburse the state and the employer for all costs incurred.

2. Every employee who has information about immoral behavior at a company or government office will be able to report this information to the corruption police in secrecy. The corruption police will investigate. If they conclude that the employer's actions are immoral but not criminal, they will transfer their findings to the media.

Chapter 38

Pensioners

In my opinion, it is counterproductive and wasteful for a business to send home automatically, every member of the workforce when that worker reaches the government's mandated retirement age, since many employees are still very productive at that age.

The following are my enumerated recommendations:

1. All citizens reaching retirement age, whether they are an employee, business owner or public servant, should have the option to continue working. In this case, the employer, in consultation with the employee and the local union representative, will have the option to decide whether to continue employing that worker, and if so, in what capacity and at what salary. However, if the employer does not wish to retain the employee after retirement age, the employer will be required to provide a valid reason.

2. Retirement age should be related to life expectancy. The ratio/difference between retirement age and life expectancy should be identical for both males and females.

3. The government should consider raising the retirement age.

4. Every citizen, including public servants, Parliament members, ministers, employees, business owners and judges, must have an identical pension plan, paying the same fixed percentage of their income, so that all citizens will be able to maintain their lifestyle after retirement (see Chapter 41: Pension Funds.)

5. Any citizen reaching retirement age should have the option of continuing payments for his or her pension fund.

6. The state should ensure that every pensioner has at least a monthly income equal to the minimum wage, even if he or she is not working, or does not have an adequate pension plan, irrespective of the reason.

Chapter 39

Public Housing and Leftover Collection

A society that allows homeless people on its streets and does not take care of them, is a society that has lost its soul! Furthermore, there are many people who cannot afford proper housing and it should be the duty of the government to help them.

It is unfortunate that the best state public housing I know of is in a non-democratic country. I am referring to Singapore. This should not mislead us into thinking that replacing democracy would be a good idea, since an enlightened dictator can be superseded by a very different leader, as was the case with Augustus in the Roman Empire who was superseded by crazy emperors like Caligula and Nero.

More recently, consider the example of a relatively enlightened leader, namely Emperor Napoleon Bonaparte. Napoleon gave France a workable governmental system (which is still used today) but he also appointed several members of his family to positions of power all over Europe, even though those family members were completely unqualified for such positions.

In "democratic" Israel, public housing is very limited, poorly managed and shrouded in secrecy. Some of the public housing is diverted to house religious institutions.

Consequently, many citizens who are eligible for public housing have to wait several years for housing or, more often than not, they never get one. While I haven't seen one homeless person in Singapore, many homeless people roam the streets in Israel, the US and other democratic countries.

Another significant issue that human society should be concerned with is food wastage. Statistically it is known that a large part of the food in the world ends up in the rubbish bin. If I invited people to eat with us, and those people left food on their plate or allowed their children to do so, I personally never invited them again. Some people claim that they cannot impose such strict discipline on their children. I claim that they are completely ignorant of how to educate children. When I decided that it was time to teach my little daughter to stop wasting food, I explained it to her. One evening she filled up her plate and left part of her food. When she insisted that she was not hungry, I put the food in the fridge and gave it to her in her next meal refusing to offer an alternative. She eventually ate the food and never again filled up her plate needlessly. Just this simple practice will reduce wastage of food significantly.

The following are my enumerated recommendations:

1. The government should provide subsidized, affordable, and well managed public housing for its citizens. This can be achieved by offering rental flats to the public for a fixed percent of their income. This way the better well off will pay higher rent and subsequently subsidize the less fortunate ones. A fixed percent of the flats in every building will be reserved for low-income earners.

2. Every building will have a percent of its flats allocated, free of charge, to homeless people.

3. All the activities of the housing department must be open to scrutiny by the public.

4. The tenants in public housing and those who are in need of public housing will rate the service in general, and in their building in particular. If the rating of a building drops below 65%, the manager will be replaced. If the rating of the governmental **housing department** drops below 65%, the department's manager will be replaced. If the problem is persistent, the **minister** in charge will be replaced.

5. By law, all food establishments, army kitchens, and all citizens should bring their leftovers to a central collection point in their neighborhood, or at least call for collection, instead of disposing of their left-over food. The needy and homeless could be used to help with the collection. This food should be used to feed the needy. This food can also be used in cheap, state-run, food establishments for the less well-off who will be employed and/or fed in these

establishments. These restaurants can also serve those who want to support these ventures. They will pay full price, and, in this way, help the homeless and unemployed to reestablish themselves.

6. The Municipality should regularly check rubbish bins for wasted food. The biometric databases will be used to penalize the offenders.

Chapter 40

Banks, Insurance Companies and Pension Funds

Banks, as you know, are an essential part of our modern economy and enable the transfer of money between suppliers, service providers and their clients. They also provide the initial finances for new businesses, among other things. **Insurance companies** exist to protect the individual who does not have the reserves to protect himself from financial disasters. **Pension funds** exist to ensure that people have enough money for their retirement age when they can no longer generate income to support themselves. However, all three perform their functions with money that the public deposits with them. This puts all three of them into a different category when compared to businesses that have to use their own finances, or the finances of their shareholders, and take the risk of failure. It is important to understand the shortcomings of the way all three institutions operate nowadays. I see seven major problems with things the way they are.

First, these institutions make huge profits for their shareholders, even though they do not have to invest in establishing the business and do not take any risks, as is the case in every other private business.

Secondly, they are strictly controlled by the government to ensure compliance with state laws. But their assets and their clients' assets are, for the most part, **not guaranteed by the government**, which means that a bankruptcy of such an establishment will cause very substantial losses to their clients. An example of the banks' lack of concern to their clients occurred some years ago when insurance companies and banks in Israel invested in several well-connected "tycoons" without proper securities. All these "tycoons" went bankrupt. Even worse, these banks assisted some of these tycoons in breaking the law. These banks were penalized financially for their grave offences. However, more importantly, many ordinary members of the public lost huge amounts of money and many people sadly lost large parts of their hard-earned pensions. But, of course, bank managers, bank employees and insurance company employees have continued to be paid their inflated salaries. Bank directors have continued to receive millions and bank shareholders have continued to receive their share of the profits. Even though the banks were heavily penalized for breaking the law, no one was prosecuted! The only losers were innocent members of the public!

Thirdly, the lack of government guarantees discourages citizens from opening accounts in new or small banks or insurance companies.

The fourth problem I have with the current situation is that banks and Insurance companies are allowed to hold excessive **market share that stifles competition.**

A fifth problem is that, at present, the public have very limited or practically no knowledge of the specific activities of these institutions even though these activities can have dire consequences on their financial well-being. As a result, greed in these major financial establishments can lead to their bankruptcy and destabilize the economy and the democratic state. For example, the great depression in Germany in the 1920's was probably due to actions of the financial establishment. This financial crisis enabled Adolf Hitler and his small party to entice desperate people to vote for him, and the rest is history.

The sixth major problem is the lack of public knowledge regarding the qualifications and the professional level of the employees in these institutions. For example, when I was living in South Africa, among my clients were large insurance companies, where I met some portfolio managers who were managing many billions of ordinary citizens' money. I naïvely expected these managers to be highly qualified. But was shocked to discover the low level of professionalism of these officials who had control over the precious life savings of many ordinary citizens.

The seventh problem I see is the result of us being conditioned to cherish our privacy which has led to allowing banks and insurance companies to operate in a confidential environment. This confidentiality benefits only crooks at the expense of honest citizens since it enables the banks and insurance companies to engage in shady practices without any direct supervision.

It is my opinion that relaxing the confidentiality will not harm the public. On the contrary, it will benefit the public by preventing these institutions from engaging in shady practices.

These are a few examples of the shortcomings in the existing system which demonstrate why we, the clients, deserve, and should have, direct control and supervision over our banks and insurance companies!

The following are my goals:

   a. Reduce the size of the different institutions, to promote competition, and prevent major catastrophes that might cause a national financial crisis. (See recommendations 11, 12.)

   b. Prevent misconduct by employees and/or collusion with rich account holders.

   c. Give the clients complete control over the operation and the quality of service. (See recommendations 2,3,4,6,7.)

   d. Make sure that all their operations are continuously visible to their clients and government inspectors.

   e. Reduce the cost of the services. (See recommendation 1.)

   f. Ideally, there should be one pension fund organization with identical conditions available to all citizens irrespective of their position. However, since it is difficult to judge how well they invest clients' money, I recommend the establishment of three competing pension funds.

The following are my enumerated recommendations:

1. Banks and insurance companies will be nonprofit organizations.
2. All these institutions will have complete online disclosure of their activities to their clients.
3. The conditions for starting a new bank or insurance company will be as follows: A person who wants to open a new bank or insurance company and become its managing director will register a new nonprofit organization, prepare a business plan, advertise for potential employees and find a potential location. Then that person

will advertise his or her business plan and proposal for potential clients, which will include a detailed CV (see Chapter 30: *Application for Employment in a Public Office*) and a certificate of approval of credentials from the national bank. The person's business plan will include a requested salary, the expected operational costs, the salaries and detailed CV's of all potential employees (see Chapter 30.) Once the person gathers enough potential clients, he or she will start operations.

4. The managing directors of all banks and insurance companies will be elected every five years by the bank's clients. The existing managing directors will publish their detailed CV's (see Chapter 30) that will include their successes and failures in the previous five years. At the same time, other applicants can also apply for this position. They will have to comply with the same conditions as required by a new managing director as described earlier.

5. All bank and insurance company employees, and particularly financial experts who make decisions regarding their clients' money, must be highly qualified in their area and be employed through public tender with all its details open to the institutions' clients.

6. All employees will be video recorded online, including voice recordings. However, the identity of the clients will be hidden with the exception of the 10% largest account holders, who will be visible to all account holders.

7. All the institution's activities, including the activities in every account, will be accessible to all the institution's clients. The identity of the account holder will be protected by codes known only to them with the exception of the largest 10% account holders, whose identity will be revealed.

8. No citizen will be allowed to hold more than one account in each bank to prevent major account holders from dividing their account and thus hiding their identity. The exposure of major account holders will prevent them from engaging in shady practices with the collusion of the bank's employees.

9. All employees in these institutions, including the managing director, similarly to every organization in the country, will receive a salary that is no more than four times the median salary in the country; with one exception (see recommendation 10.)

10. In an organization where the median salary is higher than the median salary in the country, it will be used for calculating the highest salary in this organization. This will encourage the management to reduce the discrepancies in their employees' salaries.

11. No bank can hold more than 1% of the market share.

12. Every insurance company can operate in only one insurance category and can have no more than 5% of the market share in this insurance category.

13. Every time a client receives service from a bank, insurance company or pension fund (see Chapter 41) that client will rate the service received on their internet site. This information will also be sent to the feedback organization. If the cumulative average rating of an institution drops below 65%, a new managing director will be elected by the institution's clients.

Chapter 41

Pension Funds

Pension funds are a mainstay of any employees' condition in a democratic country. However, currently the conditions of pension funds vary widely, and politicians ensure that their pension conditions far surpass the pension conditions of all other citizens. Furthermore, in some democratic countries, citizens who are not employees are not required to have pension funds. Even worse, nowadays most employees do not have enough information or control on the activities of their pension funds so that, unbeknown to them, they might not acquire the amounts that they should have had.

The following are my enumerated recommendations:

1. Pension funds will be nonprofit organizations under the jurisdiction of the government.
2. Since the conditions of all pension funds are identical, there might logically be only one pension fund organization. However, to ensure that pension money is invested in the most optimal way, three pension funds will be allowed in the country.
3. The committee that selects candidates for ministerial positions will also select managing directors for the three pension funds.
4. All pension fund employees, and particularly financial experts who make decisions regarding their clients' money, must be highly qualified in their area of expertise and be employed through a public tender with all its details open to the institutions' clients.
5. All three pension funds will publish a comparative annual report that will show their annual growth and detail all expenditures, including detailed information about the salaries of all employees and their managing directors.
6. No citizen will be allowed to hold more than one pension fund account.

7. The pension fund conditions of all citizens, including public servants, judges, ministers, and members of parliament, will be identical, so that their pensions are similarly proportionate to their income during their working years. This means that all citizens will be able to maintain a lifestyle similar to what they had during their working years.

8. All pension fund activities, including investments and clients' accounts will be easily accessible to the public. The identity of the account holders will be protected by issuing them a code known only to them. However, the identity of the 10% largest account holders will not be concealed from the rest of that institution's members.

9. All citizens will be able to transfer their pension fund to another pension fund at their discretion.

10. Every citizen will rate his or her pension fund on an annual basis. The managing director of every pension fund whose rating drops below 66% will be replaced.

Chapter 42

Stock Market

The stock market came into existence to enable organizations to expand their business using public money and enable the public to invest in much more lucrative investments, albeit with higher risk.

However, the stock market has developed into a gambling mechanism that serves very large investors and stockbrokers who make a fortune gambling with their clients' money. Moreover, many investors consider their investment as a short-term and quick money-making scheme. This consideration serves the brokers well because they make more money with all the changes in their client's investment portfolios, although this does not necessarily serve their clients well in the long term.

Furthermore, it is unreasonable that brokers are paid their commission irrespective of the success or failure of their actions. This, in my view, resulted in the current situation whereby so-called "consultants," who have never really worked hard to make a living, have lost all perspective concerning the value of money. This attitude leads them to become greedy and lose their moral compass. As a result, they work hard to promote their own interest even at the expense of their unfortunate clients. All these rapid changes in investments destabilize the stock market and make it vulnerable to crashing.

My goals in the following recommendations are to ensure that the stock market will fulfill its **intended** purpose of being a tool for long-term investment but with much more concern for the investor. **These goals are:**

 a. Enabling organizations to expand, using the public's money.
 b. Becoming a **long-term** beneficial investment for the public.
 c. Improving the chances that private investors get professional and beneficial advice.
 d. Reducing the risk of a stock market crash.
 e. Protecting the public's investment.

The following are my enumerated recommendations:

1. Selling investments in less than three months will not be allowed.
2. After three months, every investor wishing to sell an investment will receive the market price or the price of the original investment, whichever is lower. This is intended to discourage rapid changes in the investment portfolio.
3. The investor will be obliged to keep his or her investment for at least six months to get market price on that investment.
4. The investment broker who will be paid a percentage of the gains will also pay clients the same percentage of the losses. For example, if the broker's fee is 5%, the broker will receive 5% of the gains, but if the value of the investment drops, the broker will pay the investor 5% of the losses.

Chapter 43

Internet

Internet crime and fake news on the internet are the scourge of this century. Frequently we get messages which seek to gain control over our computer or cellphone. Or we receive messages intended to convince us to believe in fictitious information.

One way to have better control over these phenomena is to require every message on the internet or any other application to carry the name of the original writer, that writer's country of residence and the date of the original posting. This information of the original writer on the posting should not be affected by the number of times the message has been forwarded. A post without this information will be deleted immediately.

As a result, every fake news message, forwarded many times by unsuspecting recipients, will always show its identity, so that the recipients can better assess whether the content might be harmful, and, if necessary, will enable the authorities to prosecute.

Chapter 44

Internet Services Barter

In order to improve the quality of life of all citizens and particularly low-income ones and pensioners, I recommend that every municipality of every city will establish, in every neighborhood, a barter site for all services including internet services as well as the services of teachers, plumbers, electricians, etc. In my opinion this is an important social tool. For example, a retired teacher will teach pupils for which he or she will acquire credit hours. When the retiree needs a plumber, one will be employed in exchange for these hours.

The following are my enumerated recommendations:

1. Every Municipality will establish and manage a barter internet site at their cost and publish it to all its' residence.
2. The site will be available for every citizen and will be able to offer services and search for services the citizen requires.
3. The services offered will be on an hourly basis and free of charge. Every participant will acquire credit hours, in exchange for other services not necessarily from the same person.
4. Every user of the site will rate its performance and if the average cumulative rating of the site will drop below 65%, its manager will be replaced by the municipality.

This service will enable low-income families and/or pensioners to benefit from services without paying for them and as a result reduce their expenditure. Furthermore, it will enable pensioners to do work they are able to do and consequently stay active, meet new people, and maybe even expand their social circle.

Chapter 45

Imports and Exports

Imports and exports are the life blood of modern economies. However, imports come with some drawbacks, as they replace local products, deplete foreign currency, and are sometimes based on the exploitation of workers in the source countries.

The following are my enumerated recommendations:

1. Import licenses should be dependent on similar export licenses to the same or associated countries.
2. Import contracts must include employment conditions in the source countries and allow free access to investigators. Non-compliance will carry severe penalties. There should be a special investigative department that sends investigators to check periodically the employment conditions in the source countries.
3. Every product, including bulk products, should be clearly marked as prescribed by the government consumer agency, informing the consumer whether it is a local or imported product and identifying which country it was imported from.
4. Every imported product must have an adjacent sign advising the consumer which local product or products can be used as an alternative. In this way, consumers can consider the local alternative even if they might be paying more for it.
5. The state should promote the purchase of local products.
6. The government will ensure that the country is not dependent on the importation of critical products from non-democratic countries.

Chapter 46

Immigration and Refugees

If you find an injured poisonous snake on your doorstep and if you are a nature lover, you might take that snake for medical treatment. But even the most passionate snake lover will abstain from releasing this snake into his home with his wife and children. I believe that every democratic state should try and help refugees to the best of its abilities. But a democratic state should not be compelled to accept them, if, in its best judgment and based on previous experience, certain refugees might abuse the country's hospitality. You can read the speech by the Australian prime minister in 2021 that stated clearly that every foreigner residing in Australia must accept their values or go back to their original countries.

The following is my recommendation:

1. A democratic country should not accept individuals from countries with very strong religious beliefs and non-democratic values, even if they are refugees, unless it can be proven that these individuals have different values than those in their home countries.

Chapter 47

National and International Population Problems

The world population is experiencing two contradictory processes. On the one hand, there is a world population explosion, while on the other hand the population in all rich democratic countries is decreasing rapidly. This situation creates two problems: In the poor Third World countries there is rampant poverty and neglect of the population. In the developed countries, a lack of manpower and lack of income from the younger generation to support the pensions of the older generation puts the social security system at great risk.

You might say that the problems are being solved by the refugees and immigrants that arrive in the developed countries. I believe that they do not solve but create problems. We see today that European countries suffer from crime, religious intolerance and creation of *no-go* areas in their cities, all created by uneducated immigrants and refugees with different core values and religions who fail to assimilate into the society of their host countries.

In my opinion there is a different way to solve, or at least alleviate, the problem of the rapidly declining birthrate in developed countries, while helping Third World countries far more than monetary donations. Furthermore, it might reduce the population in the Third World and consequently all over the world.

The following are my enumerated recommendations:

1. Every rich nation will enter into agreements with one or more poor nations to sponsor small cities or villages, by investing in their infrastructure and improving their educational system. This will ensure that the younger generation will finish high school with a similar education and similar core values like their counterparts in the country that has sponsored them.

2. When these young people graduate from high school at the age of 18, the sponsoring country will select an agreed upon percentage of these high school graduates. These young people will then be able to immigrate and join the work force or enter higher educational institutions in the sponsoring country to supplement their educated work force.

3. For this scheme to work successfully the sponsoring country must select only Third World countries, whose culture and religion is not antagonistic to its own democratic and religious values.

Chapter 48

Foreign Aid

Every western country allocates large amounts of money for foreign aid. I wonder how many US citizens would have agreed to send so much financial aid to Israel, had they known that the Israeli army employs a general who is a religious professional, as well as hundreds if not thousands of religious food supervisors. These supervisors are employed despite the fact that this same food has already been supervised by many more religious supervisors in the food factories and on the farms. Moreover, if US citizens had known that probably 20-30% of the Israeli national government and municipal budgets are allocated to support parasitic religious communities for political reasons, they would have never agreed to send money to Israel instead of using it for needy local people.

Similarly, many democratic countries support Third World countries without making sure that the money does not disappear into the pockets of corrupt officials, which is unfortunately very often the case.

I believe that citizens should have a say in how much money will be allocated for foreign aid, instead of using this money for social security, social services, improving infrastructure, or other important uses in their own country.

The following are my enumerated recommendations:

1. Before the government decides on its foreign aid budget, every citizen will receive a short report listing the amounts allocated for foreign aid for each country and the reasons for these allocations. This will be accompanied by a short report published by the media, expressing their opinions about these foreign aid allocations.
2. All citizens will write the amount of aid that they think should be allocated to each foreign country and submit their report through the internet.

3. The average amount of foreign aid suggested by all the citizens for each foreign country will be used as a guideline for government spending on foreign aid. If the government deviates from this recommended average amount to any one foreign country it will be obliged to justify its reasons for this deviation.
4. Foreign aid will always be in the form of products and services from the donating country and never with actual cash.

Chapter 49

Gambling

Although we all know that gambling causes much harm to some members of our society and to their families, it would not be practical to eliminate it altogether. We all know that the American government's attempt at alcohol prohibition, with all its good intentions, failed miserably, with disastrous consequences. However, the government should attempt to reduce the disastrous impact that habitual gambling has on many people's lives by actively trying to discourage gambling. The government should provide gambling facilities for the public while limiting its impact on individuals.

The following are my enumerated recommendations:

1. The government should provide gambling facilities. These facilities should display warnings signs, emphasizing the dangers of gambling. Furthermore, government employees working in these facilities should be trained to try and discourage people from excessive gambling.

2. Any form of direct or indirect advertising which encourages gambling, whether by private organizations or the government, should be prohibited.

3. The maximum prize, awarded by the government's gambling organization, should not exceed ten year's median annual income. The organization should award as many prizes as possible. Reducing the maximum prize will hopefully reduce the number of gamblers who believe that the prize will change their lives.

4. Most of the proceeds of the government's gambling organization will be distributed to the winners. A percentage of the proceeds should be put towards publications warning about the dangers of gambling, and a small percentage will be used for the actual cost of the operation.

5. Every citizen, whose income is **below the national median income**, will be required to contact the income tax office who will specify the amount that he or she is allowed to spend on gambling every month/year. The tax office will implement a system similar to a credit card, whereby the tax office will directly limit the amount the citizen is allowed to spend on gambling every month/year in all gambling institutions. I suggest that the amount allowed for gambling will not exceed 25% of the citizen's net income.

6. All public and private gambling institutions, including casinos, will have a direct link to the tax office. The tax office will restrict the amount that the citizen can spend on gambling in all establishments.

7. Every citizen will be required to present an ID in every gambling establishment, so that the establishment can confirm with the tax office how much that citizen is allowed to gamble.

8. When the cumulative monthly or annual amount allowed is reached, the citizen will not be allowed to gamble until the end of that period.

I know that my suggestions do not sound democratic. However, how democratic is it for us to allow a citizen to destroy his or her life by gambling, and then demand money from the state's social services? Why should the public finance the cost of helping gamblers who have destroyed their own and their families' lives?

Chapter 50

Prostitution

Prostitution will not disappear, and it causes no harm except to the women practicing it, if it is not managed and regulated properly.

It is ludicrous that actresses that perform explicit sexual acts onscreen are revered and paid handsomely but prostitutes that supply similar but essential service to lonely men are despised. This was not so from the beginning of history and is another despicable contribution that the monotheistic religions brought to our lives. This attitude brought untold misery to the lives of so many women that could not otherwise support themselves. To put things in perspective, a prostitute can service one or two clients a day and earn more than a similarly unqualified woman that works full time as a cashier in a supermarket. And who are we to judge what a respectable profession is and what isn't? Once musicians and actors were considered as the lowest in society. Today they are revered. There were long periods in Europe that courtesans were respected women, even though they supplied sex for financial support. Josephine, later Napoleon's wife, was one of them.

Therefore, prostitution should be legal, and practiced in the same way as any other paramedical profession.

The following are my enumerated recommendations:

1. Prostitutes will be treated and regulated in the same way as any other paramedical profession and service, like massage or physiotherapy.
2. Prostitutes will have to pass regular medical tests to prevent sexually transmitted diseases.
3. Living off the proceeds of a prostitute will be criminalized and heavily penalized.
4. Every prostitute will be able to work independently or rent an office in a private paramedical office building, with all the rights and obligations as any other practitioner of the paramedical profession in the country.

Chapter 51

Alternative United Nations Organization

The United Nations was created with very good intentions and serves a very important role. However, since most of its members are non-democratic countries, it has completely lost its moral standing and its effectiveness is partial at best. One glaring example is the fact that Israel has been condemned more than all the non-democratic countries combined, and more than countries that promote terrorism. It is expected that such an institution will deal with issues like terrorism, corruption, racism, inequality, etc. more vigorously than it does currently. My hope is that an alternative institution on the following principles will be able to better fulfill such goals.

The following are my enumerated recommendations:

1. All the democratic countries should establish an alternative UN organization. This UN organization will be open to all nations who wish to be members, but only democratic nations will be given **voting rights**.

2. All the **appointments** in such an organization should be filled by individuals from democratic countries.

3. In order to entice Third World countries to join, foreign aid will be given only to nations that have joined the Alternative UN organization.

4. All foreign aid should be in the form of projects, which will be carried out by companies from the donor country. Foreign aid should never be in the form of financial aid.

5. One of the first duties of this organization should be to redesign the internet in order to reduce its vulnerability to crime, to establish clear rules, and to compel every new software or application to be designed in such a way that will prevent misuse of the internet.

Every country that will join this system will have to abide by these rules. This will, at last, stop the patchwork that is the main reason for the shortcomings of the existing internet system.

Chapter 52

Citizen's Duties

In the previous 51 chapters you have seen all the changes that, in my opinion, are required to make the state truly democratic and give you, the citizen, control and supervision over the activities of the public service and private enterprise. However, you have noticed that protecting your rights and interests will require your perpetual involvement.

One day while working on this book, my girlfriend, while reading the draft of this book suddenly said: "Adam, you really expect the citizens in your ideal state to keep themselves busy with so many tasks?"

I replied: "Do you remember what you said eight months ago when I told you that you must weigh yourself daily and also weigh the food you eat? You thought that this was insane. Now, 8 months later and 8 kilograms less, you feel great, and you do not consider this to be a trouble at all. Similarly, the citizens in my ideal democratic state, once they get used to being involved and reap the benefits, will not be able to think about living in any other way."

You should remember all the time what Greek philosopher Plato said already thousands of years ago: "The price good men pay for indifference to public affairs is to be ruled by evil men."

The following is a summary of all the duties you will have, duties which will give you comprehensive participation in the running of your democratic country and will ensure that the government works for you and that the private enterprise gives you the best of service and takes care of your interests. (I am referencing a Parliamentary system, but the following duties can also be adjusted to apply to other forms of democracy such as the US system of government.)

Each of the following duties is detailed in the relevant chapter. Keep in mind that most of your duties have to be fulfilled only once every five years!

The following is a summary of your duties:

1. From the comfort of your home, vote every five years for Parliament. Choose your favorite party, and number their members in

order of preference, after reading their resumes or curriculum vitae. If you vote for a marginal party, add your second and third choice.

2. Vote every five years for the candidates for a **25 member professional committee**, which will select the **candidates for ministers in the 12 ministerial offices**.
3. Vote every five years for the new **comptroller general**.
4. Vote every five years for the **head of the national legal system** which will be independent of the government.
5. Vote every five years for the **head of the legal services office**.
6. Vote every five years for the **national police chief** and **national prosecutor**.
7. Vote every five years for the **police chief and chief prosecutor in your city or county**.
8. Vote every five years for your candidate for the **head of the corruption police force** and **prosecutor**.
9. Vote every five years for the **manager of the feedback organization**.
10. Elect every five years your **bank and insurance company managing directors**.
11. Read 1-2 page summary of the important news every 1-2 months, and then answer a short questionnaire.
12. Read a daily newspaper.
13. Proudly wear your name tag on your chest.
14. Tell the whole truth when questioned by a policeman or a lawyer who is representing you and similarly tell the whole truth in court.
15. Vote annually for, or against, the inclusion of medical services and medicines in the list of approved services and medications.
16. Rate every business, bank, insurance company, government office, police official and judges every time you use their services. Not only negative experiences will be recorded but also positive ones. Otherwise, in our new democracy, managing directors and government officials will be replaced too frequently, and maybe needlessly.

Chapter 53

Epilogue

The democratic system, while undoubtedly the best governmental system invented by humanity, has its flaws due to its idealistic principles, its implementation, and the shortcomings of human nature. As a result, the life of citizens in most democratic countries is not as satisfying as it could be. In addition, the system, as it is being implemented nowadays, is extremely vulnerable to anti-democratic forces, which, in many instances, use the liberal values of the democratic system to **take over the country**. These anti-democratic leaders use their newly acquired power to subvert and destroy the existing democratic system. Two very well-known examples of this phenomenon are Adolf Hitler in Germany and Benito Mussolini in Italy. More recently we saw how Turkey, Poland, Hungary and Bangladesh lost their democracy. However, these are not the only examples in modern times, which illustrate how democratic countries are in danger of becoming non-democratic through systematic blatant abuse of the democratic system. Other examples of this dangerous process are the 14 nations that were formerly part of the Soviet Union. These nations achieved their independence in 1990-91, and five of them are already fully fledged dictatorships.

Furthermore, Israel in its 80 years of existence is a recent and glaring example of the vulnerability of every democratic state to becoming non-democratic. Following persecution in modern times, mostly secular and atheist Jews settled in Palestine, and established the new state of Israel in 1948, based on democratic principles, despite fierce resistance from **many religious Jews who insisted on waiting for the Messiah**. These religious Jews continued subverting the democratic system by using their unified voting power and high birth rate, and as a result, after only seventy-five years, Israel has become a very fragile democracy **with religious control over most aspects of daily life.**

How did this happen that Israel is losing its democracy?

The founding fathers succeeded in making Israel a prosperous nation. However, they made some serious mistakes which tarnished their huge achievement. They did not create a constitution. Moreover, they discriminated against people who were not members of the ruling party, and this led to widespread nepotism. As a result, corruption became endemic in all aspects of society. Other mistakes pertained to the religious minority in Israel. The founding fathers did not separate between religion and state (the only democratic country in the world who failed to do so.) They also enabled a small group of religious zealots to occupy themselves with full time religious studies, while receiving full financial support from the state. Moreover, the government financed religious schools while relinquishing all supervision over them and also the government subsidized infants.

As a result, the religious Jews have the highest birth rate in the country and the majority of men in the religious community do not receive proper education and therefore do not have the educational and financial ability to support themselves and their families. Instead, many of them occupy themselves with religious studies, while relying on state subsidies. And, if this is not bad enough, their high birth rate increased their political power. This increased power has enabled them to establish a religious ministry which has been able to finance numerous religious activities and religious positions of power. In addition, the government has generously subsidized families with children, enabling the religious community to have very large families, which has radically changed the demography of Israeli society.

These religious zealots are also represented in parliament. They vote as a block and always for their religious leaders. Even if these leaders have been prosecuted for corruption, they are allowed to return to serve in Parliament and even as ministers in the same ministerial position. Now that these religious leaders are in government, they are able to extort huge amounts of money from the government purse and municipal budgets in various ways, including financing tens-of-thousands of religious positions at the taxpayers' expense. Furthermore, these religious Jews have a substantial impact on the cost of living, and, in fact, they have control over all aspects of life in Israel.

We can identify four main ways that powerful, incompetent, and corrupt political leaders can undermine, and eventually destroy the democratic system:

1. Eliminating humanities from the educational system, and/or using the educational system to indoctrinate school pupils. This produces school graduates who are incapable of an intelligent and objective evaluation of their government. This results in these young people blindly following their charismatic and powerful leaders, with very dangerous consequences.
2. Allowing powerful religious leaders to coerce their followers to vote en masse for their choice of candidate and/or party.
3. Giving religious leaders the power to control the educational system of their followers, as is the case in Israel, so that these youngsters cannot acquire the necessary skills to support themselves, and, as a result, have to rely on their politicians to extort state funding for them.
4. Replacing public servants in key positions by incompetent cronies.

Even in the US, we see signs of danger to American democracy. Firstly, the American voting system historically put the emphasis on the rights of states. As a result, citizens have less direct influence on the central government. Secondly, because candidates for office rely on donations, it is inevitable that they will be prejudiced in favor of their wealthy donors. Thirdly, even though separation between church and state is guaranteed in the constitution, this separation is being eroded. An example of this is the success of "the right to life" movement, which is objecting to abortions, based on their religious beliefs, and succeeding in imposing strict limitations on women's rights.

As a result of the serious flaws in the American legislative system, President Barack Obama was prevented from implementing most of his ideas which would have benefited the public, like medical aid to all, which is available in almost all democratic countries and even in some non-democratic countries like Cuba.

Furthermore, the vulnerability of American democracy was dramatically exposed, when on January 6, 2021, following President Donald Trump's defeat in the presidential elections, his supporters attacked the United States Capitol Building in Washington, D.C. The mob sought to keep Trump in power. Suddenly, it became clear that the most powerful democracy in the world is in danger! This dangerous process can reach a threshold, beyond which it is irreversible, until the democratic state is doomed.

Shockingly, the US is rated today as a **flawed democracy**, along with Israel and South Africa.

We can conclude that corruption in general, and religious indoctrination in particular, has destroyed many nations and empires, and you should be in no doubt that it can destroy your country's democracy.

Now that you have read my book, what are you going to do about saving your country from the threat of these dangerous anti-democratic forces?

I believe that the proposals in my book will make ordinary citizens like you more involved in running the country, will improve your quality of life, and will ensure the continued existence of the democratic system in your country.

This book is intended to start the discussion and is a call to action for citizens in democratic countries who are the victims of the shortcomings in the existing democratic system—a system which principally serves politicians, the rich and powerful, and large corporations, rather than the overwhelming majority of the population.

If I have convinced you that we need to take action, be warned! The road to change will not be easy, as it will encounter resistance from all the groups that currently benefit from it, at your expense. This change will have to be implemented slowly and gradually from within the existing democratic system. But it will be worth it in the end as it will result in a much healthier society, and one which is less vulnerable to becoming non-democratic.

GOOD LUCK !

Appendix

Appendix 1: *Example of Calculating the Reduction of Parliament Members for All Parties When the Number of Parliament Members of the Winning Party Has Been Increased*

See Chapter 6: *Parliamentary System*

If for example, the winning party received 40% in the first elections, all the other parties had 60% in the first elections. But now they must be reduced to 49% then the redaction coefficient will be 49/60=0.8166. This coefficient will be used to calculate the new reduced number of the members in all the other parties excluding the winning party.

The winning party in the second elections will have its percent of votes increased to 51% and consequently will have 61 out of 120 members in Parliament.

All the other parties' members will be reduced accordingly.

The calculation will be as follows:

For example:

If the other parties had 30%, 20% and 10% = total of 60%

This must be reduced from 60% to 49%.

First, we have to calculate the reduction coefficient:

49/60 = 0.8166

Second, we have to calculate the new percent each party will have:

30% X 0.8166 = 24.498%

20% X 0.8166 = 16.332%

10% X 0.8166 = 8.166%

Total 48.996 = 49%

They will have the following number of parliament members:

24.498% of 120 = 29.39 = 29 parliament members

16.332% of 120 = 19.59 = 20 parliament members

8.166% of 120 = 9.79 = 10 parliament members

Total number of parliament members, excluding the leading party = 59 of the total of 120.

Appendix 2 : *My Experience With the Israeli Military Legal System—A Soldier's Experience*

See Chapter 17: *Courts and Judges—The legal System*

After my compulsory army service in the Israeli army, I was called to serve in the reserve forces during one of the wars with terrorists in Lebanon.

I was posted at the border with Lebanon. My duty was to help the military police in preventing smuggling by Israeli soldiers from Lebanon to Israel. A truck arrived. We stopped it, and I went with the driver to check that there were no smuggled goods on the truck. When checking a storage compartment underneath the truck I noticed hidden video recording machines. I turned around and saw the barrel of a sub machine gun pointed at my face.

"You forget what you saw or die," he uttered.

What the smuggling Israeli soldier did not know was that I was well trained in karate and giving in to bullying was against my nature. However, I was rational enough to realize what interrogation I will face had I killed him. I pushed the barrel of the gun with my left hand and pulled him close to me with the right and stood there a second pondering the situation.

This was not a situation that allowed the slightest mistake; this gun pointed towards me could fire; one second and that would be the end of me. I kept holding him close to me with my right hand while pushing the barrel of the gun with my left hand and pushing him backwards until we came into view of the rest of the military police.

We arrested him. I did not know then that this had been the easy part. Now I faced the realities of the military legal system.

Before I testified in court, I found out that the smuggling soldier belonged to a criminal organization and that I could face retributions. I talked to the prosecutor and requested him to make sure that the accused would not know my address. He promised me to do so! The "word of a lawyer."

In court, the judge asked for my name and address. I looked at the prosecutor and he looked the other way. I had no choice. I said my name and address watching the grinning face of the accused.

The most important point for our discussion is that the defense lawyer's "line of defense" was that I was lying: "Because no one in his right mind would do what I said I did with a barrel of a submachine gun pointed towards his face."

Later I received threatening phone calls to my flat. I had a wife and a baby daughter.

I found the address of the criminal, observed his home, and vowed that if he touches my family, I will burn his house down with him and his family inside.

Luckily, he did not pursue his vendetta and I and my family went on with our lives.

This is only one small example of how the life of every one of us can be destroyed because of the current legal system. This also reflects on the daily realities of every policeman. That's why we must understand the pressures every policeman has to deal with every day when each officer is putting their life on the line protecting us from chaos.

Appendix 3: *How a Banker Used His Financial Power to Avoid Paying a Supplier*

See Chapter 10 : *The Legal Services Office*

I encountered another glaring example of the unjust legal system when a friend of mine, a former client, who used to be the financial director of a finance company, had started developing software for banks. He told me that previously he had not been paid for his software, but now he had a sponsor. So, he felt reassured that if a bank will again refuse to pay him for his product, he would be able to fight back. Once again, the bank did not pay him. So, my friend turned to his sponsor. However, his sponsor did nothing to help him since the initial legal costs amounted to a million Rand! My friend had no choice but to give up.

Appendix 4: *An Israeli Lawyer's Version of the Contingency System*

See Chapter 10: *The Legal Services Office*

The following is my personal experience with an Israeli lawyer and the contingency system: I was forced to return to Israel because of the deteriorating economical and personal safety situation in South Africa, following the fall of the apartheid government. Failing to find employment in Israel, I considered starting a consulting business there. My proposed business was to be based on the contingency system, whereby I am paid based on results. This would be similar to my previous business in South Africa. From my previous experience with Israeli mentality, I was skeptical with regard to my chances of being paid for my services.

However, I consulted with an Israeli Industrial Engineer who employed me in the past. His response was: "In Israel no one will pay you a percent of the savings you achieved for him."

Out of desperation I approached a lawyer and offered him to work on a contingency system, whereby, I will pay him a percent of the company's income and in return he will recover non payments at his cost.

He agreed! He then prepared an agreement between us and gave it to me to sign. However, I am capable of reading a legal document. His contract specified that I would pay him a percent of my income in perpetuity. His obligations were not mentioned at all in the contract!

I asked him: "Where are your obligations?"

He replied: "Don't you trust me? I will not specify my obligations in writing!"

Appendix 5: *The Diet Industry as an Example for the Need for Better Government Supervision*

See Chapter 36: *Private Organizations*

I am not an expert on diets and healthy living! However, I decided to share with you my personal experience in this regard. My experience will demonstrate the futility in believing the promises of the diet industry and the urgent need for better public, and government supervision on private companies in general and the diet industry in particular.

The following is based on the book *Just Not a Diet!* by Leah Reznikovich, published in Hebrew in 2009, and on my personal experience.

It is well documented that most diets fail in the short or medium term, and they can also result in adverse effects on health.

Despite the above, there is a huge industry of methods offering to reduce weight. Therefore, it is crucial to enforce regulation and supervision on their long term success rates and possible adverse health consequences. Therefore, every consultant or business offering products or consultation with regard to weight loss should be required to inform potential clients about the long-term effects which their methods have had on previous clients.

In my opinion, the only viable method of reducing weight and maintaining good health is cost-free and gradual change of your eating habits. Since obesity, in most cases, is a mental and not physical problem, your diet should cost you nothing.

You should acquire two new best friends: a scale next to your bed, to weigh yourself every morning and record your weight in a diary, and a scale in your kitchen to weigh the food that you eat.

You should weigh your food every time you eat and try gradually to reduce the total weight in your meal and total weight of the food you eat in a day. However, if you are healthy, don't avoid eating whatever you enjoy.

Look at what you eat and try gradually to change the ingredients to healthy ones. You must always make sure that you enjoy your food and not develop cravings. When you do eat unhealthy foods, enjoy it; just try to reduce the amounts.

Eat slowly, prolong chewing your food, put a small amount on your plate and, only if you feel further cravings, should you eat some more.

There is no difficulty in finding online recipes which are easy and tasty. And there is no difficulty in finding online healthy replacements for fatty foods.

Also, it is extremely important to take daily, fast-paced walks. Only if you return home sweating will you know that you served your body well.

Try to reduce eating out. Meeting with friends can be over a cup of coffee and not a big meal. When eating at home you know the ingredients in your food, whereas, to make tasty food and do so cheaply, restaurants must use excessive amounts of sugar, salt and fat, all of which are unhealthy in excessive amounts.

I enjoy the food I make so much that I almost never eat out. When I leave home for a few hours, I always take with me a small, tasty sandwich and a thermos with chicory (coffee replacement.)

And here quietly, when nobody is listening, I must confess my sins: I crave sweet things, and I don't avoid them altogether. In the evening when the cravings reach their height, I do munch a bit on chocolate. I hold the chocolate cube in my mouth as long as I can and cherish the taste for a long time. And if I exaggerate, my best friend next to my bed reminds me of my sins in the morning.

If most of your food is healthy and only 20-30% is unhealthy and you enjoy it, then you have achieved your dieting goal.

And when you do break your diet on occasions, enjoy it, weigh yourself the next morning, and go back to the better habits you acquired.

Don't be impatient, and do not expect or try to get drastic reductions in your weight. Losing one kilogram in a week, or a month, or six months is a nice achievement.

Maintaining the above recommendations, I was able to reduce my weight over the years from 87 to 75 kilograms and maintain a perfect health at the age of 73. Today, I still try to lose one or two more kilograms, but this is driven only by vanity. I crave the pleasure of exposing my "six-pack" fully.

Appendix 6: *Lack of Consideration for Human Engineering*

See Chapter 36: *Private Organizations*

In order to further clarify some of the shortcomings of the high-tech industry, I would like to share with you two of my personal experiences in this regard.

"Once upon a time," when I entered an organisation intending on improving its efficiency, I collected all the paper forms in order to eliminate duplications. Then, I took each redesigned paper form to the worker who had to use it, handed it to him, and left. Later, I returned and asked the worker if he was satisfied.

If he was not, I told myself, "Adam you failed! Redesign the form so that it will be clearer and easier for the worker to use it." It was completely clear to me and to every engineer graduating from university that a design must consider the person or worker using it.

Contrary to the above example, contemporary designers in the high-tech industry treat their clients with contempt. They conveniently assume that it is the client's fault if he or she fails to use their products. I would love to make all these high-tech geniuses overhaul the engine of their car before they use it or fix the compressor before they store food in their fridge.

I had the displeasure of checking some computer systems, realising that a lot of things were not considered. As a result, the software does not give solutions to many instances that occur in real life. A software "genius" wrote it without much understanding of the real requirements of the user.

www.ingramcontent.com/pod-product-compliance
Lightning Source LLC
Chambersburg PA
CBHW072236270326
41930CB00010B/2147